The President's Series

in Arkansas and Regional Studies

volume three

Mark Noble, Second Arkansas Cavalry.
Photo courtesy of Barbara Thurmond.

Portraits of Conflict

A PHOTOGRAPHIC HISTORY
OF ARKANSAS
IN THE CIVIL WAR

Bobby Roberts and Carl Moneyhon

The University of Arkansas Press

Fayetteville   1987

Copyright © 1987 by
The Board of Trustees of the University of Arkansas
The University of Arkansas Press, Fayetteville, Arkansas
All rights reserved
Printed and bound in Japan

Designer: Chiquita Babb
Typeface: Linotron 202 Fournier
Typesetter: G & S Typesetters, Inc.
Printer: Dai Nippon Printing Co., Ltd.
Binder: Dai Nippon Printing Co., Ltd.

The paper used in this publication meets the minimum
requirements of the American National Standard for
Permanence of Paper for Printed Library Materials
Z39.48-1984. ⊗

Library of Congress Cataloging-in-Publication Data

Roberts, Bobby Leon
    Portraits of conflict.

    Bibliography: p.
    Includes index.
    1. Arkansas—History—Civil War, 1861–1865—
Pictorial works.   2. United States—History—
Civil War, 1861–1865—Pictorial works.
I. Moneyhon, Carl H., 1944–   II. Title.
E496.9.R63   1987   973.7'09767   87-5869
ISBN 0-938626-83-3
ISBN 0-938626-84-1 (pbk.)

To those men
who photographed the Civil War in Arkansas

Acknowledgments

In producing this book the authors have incurred many obligations. We have received help and encouragement from a great number of individuals and institutions. We would like to thank in particular Linda Pine, Rebecca Bowman, Jessie Wallace, and Joy Geisler on the staff of the University of Arkansas at Little Rock Archives and Special Collections. John Ferguson, Russell Baker, and Lynn Ewbank, photograph archivist, at the Arkansas History Commission were of inestimable help. Mary Medearis of the South Arkansas Regional Archives and Don Montgomery of the Old Washington State Park provided assistance in locating photographs from the southwestern part of the state.

The staffs of the following institutions also gave us considerable help: The United States Naval Audio Visual Center, the Western History Collection at the University of Oklahoma, the Washington County Historical Society, Henderson State University Museum, the Springfield-Greene County Library District, the Missouri Historical Society, the National Archives, the Library of Congress, the Museum of the Confederacy, the Public Library of Camden and Ouachita County, the State Historical Society of Missouri, the Kansas State Historical Society, the Arkansas Historical Association, the Old State House Museum, the Public Library of Cincinnati and Hamilton County, the Special Collections of the University of Arkansas at Fayetteville Library, the State Historical Society of Iowa, and the Illinois State Historical Society.

Many individuals very graciously shared their private collections and their personal photographs. We would like to thank particularly Barbara Thurmond, Lucille Rogers, Pamela Manning Fein, Mrs. Frank J. Wilson, Bill Rasp, Roger Davis, Dale Kirkman, Martha Ramseur Gillham, Tim Sisk, Mrs. Ralph Porter, David Perdue, Tami Tidwell, Greg McMahon, Lawrence T. Jones, Gary Hendershott, and Michael Polston. We also appreciate the contributions of the students in the Civil War history class at the University of Arkansas at Little Rock in the spring of 1984 who prepared biographies of several of the Confederate soldiers used in this book.

We would like to thank Miller Williams, Sandy Reyes, and Brenda Zodrow of the University of Arkansas Press for their encouragement of this project and wonderful production work done by the Press.

A very special debt is owed to Pat Purnell-Grauer and Jon LeMay. Jon copied many of the photographs gathered in the initial stages of the project, and Pat worked diligently to produce camera quality prints for the text.

Contents

Portraits of Conflict

Introduction

Photography, Arkansas, and the Civil War

The American Civil War was the first conflict fought under the intensive scrutiny of the camera. When the war broke out, the art of capturing images on metal plates and paper was a little over twenty years old. Louis Jacques Mandé Daguerre had introduced the first practical process of fixing images from life upon copper plates only in 1839. The new art form had gained ready acceptance throughout the United States. In the twenty years that intervened between 1839 and the outbreak of the American Civil War, photography had made great advances. Perhaps the most noteworthy, because it made possible the activities of many of the wartime photographers, was the development in 1851 of the wet-plate process. This new technique gave photographers greater flexibility and allowed them to establish the mobile studios that appeared during the war. While still a clumsy and difficult process, photography had developed technically by 1861 to the point that it could capture the images of the American struggle.

For the photographer, the war presented the first opportunity to capture thousands of portraits of the young men who flocked eagerly to combat. Daguerrotypists, ambrotypists, melainotypists, and those using their new wet plate process photographed the soldiers of both the North and South in their new military clothing. Those young men posed in the midst of elaborate scenes, holding equipment specially provided by the photographer. Throughout the war, America's soldiers continued to sit before the cameras. One of the greatest legacies left by the war was a vast bequest of individual photographs.

A few photographers, however, saw the war as a much greater opportunity. Mathew G. Brady, one of the nation's foremost portrait photographers and photographic innovators, envisioned documenting the war with the camera. Brady began his monumental work in the summer of 1861 after receiving permission to accompany the Union army in the field. He and his assistants recorded the battlefield of First Bull Run, and

3

Brady became so involved that he was almost captured. Before the war was over, Brady and his assistants had made thousands of pictures. Ultimately his idea of chronicling the war was copied by the numerous competitors who joined him in the field. The most noteworthy of these was Alexander Gardner who left Brady in 1863 to set up his own studio.

The United States government employed several photographers during the war, although usually on a contract basis. Gardner, for example, was employed by the secret service and copied maps. Others provided documentation of the works of the army's various branches, particularly the engineers and quartermaster corps. Captain A. J. Russell recorded the work of the engineers with the Army of the Potomac. The government hired another photographer, George M. Barnard, to provide scenes of the construction of Sherman's lines at Atlanta in September and October of 1864. Samuel A. Cooley followed Sherman's Tenth Corps from Savannah to Charleston with a contract to photograph military installations. Other photographers worked for the Union army under such arrangements, but the number is not known.

West of the Mississippi River, few photographers were concerned with the war. As a result, the legacy is small when compared to that of the eastern theaters. Among the exceptions were A. D. Lytle, a Confederate photographer at Baton Rouge, and J. D. Edwards of New Orleans, although most of Edwards' work was done in Florida. Most of those who worked in the West were portrait photographers, little interested in reproducing actual war scenes. Yet they did leave a small testament in the form of outdoor photographs. Like the work of their eastern counterparts, the western photographers provided additional insights into war—the concrete images that go beyond the words of the leaders and soldiers. They cast new light on what has been called the dark corner of the Civil War conflict.

Of all that occurred during the Civil War, the events that took place in Arkansas are the least known. Even compared with its neighbor, Louisiana, the photographic record is small. Such a record does exist, however. In Arkansas, photographic work had pushed into the state just prior to the war. The 1860 census, on the eve of the war, lists nineteen daguerrotypists in the state. Their advertisements indicate that they were quite current in their techniques and in their equipment. J. Nelson advertised his Helena studio in 1860 as able to offer "ambrotypes, melainotypes, vignette ambrotypes, and meliographs."[1] Nelson also provided coloring in his photographs. We know very little of these photographers other than the fact that there were enough of them to record the faces of many Arkansans as they went off to war.

Arkansas photographers experienced a business boom when newly recruited Confederate Arkansans rushed to have their likenesses made in their military regalia. One of the first stops of the freshly sworn-in soldier was at the studio of a portrait photographer so that an image could be made to be sent home to his family and friends. Sir Henry Morton Stanley, encamped with the Sixth Arkansas Infantry Regiment remembered, "We bought long Colt's revolvers, and long-bladed bowie-knives; we had our images taken in tin-types in our war-paint and most ferocious aspects, revolver in one hand, bowie-knife in the other, and a most portentous scowl between the eyebrows."[2] The Confederate view of the war, for Arkansas, is comprised of such portraits.

The Federal blockade brought an early end to activities of Southern photographers. The war cut off their chemicals and other supplies. The large number of photographs of Confederates made at the beginning quickly dwindled. As early as January 22, 1862, A. L. Warner at Washington in Hempstead County advertised:

Not Blockaded, My Picture Gallery is again opened and a good selection of cases in hand. Those who desire Types either of themselves or friends would do well to make an early application, as my present stock of material will soon be consumed, and no more to be had except at exorbitant prices.[3]

Confederate newspapers in 1863, 1864, and 1865 reflected the drying up of sources, as photographers' advertisements virtually disappeared.

Some studios remained in operation, however, and Arkansas Confederates flocked to them whenever possible. Junius Bragg reported on a visit that he made to the Le Roser Picture Gallery in Shreveport in April, 1864. He wrote to his wife:

The Gallery was a little den of a place with its sides covered with old faded blue cambric, and two little rickety screens. The floor was of pine slabs, as well as I could judge through the stratum of dirt and wash, which had been apparently accumulating for the past half dozen years. There were fifteen soldiers ahead of us, who were going to have their 'picture took.' As each one brought from one to four friends with him, to see the operation, they made quite a sizable little crowd, in the 'Gallery' which was not sixteen feet square. All these men had their Ambrotypes taken in the same jacket—a black one, with blue collar. Eleven of the number, had a large old rusty 'Navy six shooter' in their hands, which made the warriors look very sanguinary. No doubt their friends will think they are all well uniformed and all armed with pistols. They all wet their long ambrosial locks and slicked them down, so as to look 'gay and festive' . . . [Mine] is not a good picture, and as I never did get a good one, I do not think I am one of those who take well. I only paid forty dollars for it.[4]

The vacuum created by the disappearance of Confederate photographers was filled as Union troops moved into the state. Many Northern photographers accompanied the invading armies.

Just as their Confederate counterparts had done, most of these specialized in individual portraits, but they continued to provide an occasional outdoor view. Toward the end of the war, the Quartermaster Corps hired some of them to document the construction that had taken place. The photographs of outdoor scenes, while rare, provide the best insight into the Civil War in Arkansas and how it was fought.

The number of photographers who worked in Arkansas during the war is not known. In many cases, the only record we have of their names comes from the back of their works, in particular *cartes de visite* and postcards produced for the troops. Unfortunately, many of these did not have the names of their establishments stamped on the back. In Pine Bluff, Habicht & Mealy provided photographs. Clay & Brothers at Fort Smith offered to take "pictures of Abraham's soldiers in the latest and most improved style known to art."[5]

Many photographers worked in Little Rock after its fall in September, 1863. Brown's Gallery, Slatter's, Mansfield and Hand, R. H. White, Eaton and Mansfield, and Thomas W. Bankes all operated in the city at some time during the war. They offered ambrotypes, ferrotypes, and photographs. Slatter charged $2.50 per dozen for card pictures, "Northern prices, and (a thing hitherto unattained in Little Rock), Northern style."[6] Eaton and Mansfield advertised their great "multiplying machine, which makes *two to twenty-five* pictures at one sitting,"[7] this enabling them to furnish all at the very lowest prices.

Little is known of these men, Confederate or Federal. Of all the photographers, information about their lives could be found on only two. The Federal photographer R. H. White had a studio at De Valls Bluff where, in addition to portraits, he provided some of the most graphic photographs of scenes in Arkansas during the war. He moved on to Little Rock after the occupation where he became one of the few photographers favored by a government contract. His most impressive outdoor work would be done for the Quartermaster Corps at Little Rock where near the end of the war he documented the government construction in the city.

Another photographer, Thomas W. Bankes, is the one photographer of whom there is any extensive information, although even he is elusive. He worked both at Helena and at Little Rock. Bankes was a prolific picture taker, and left the largest collection of Arkansas photographs. At Helena he chronicled not only its individual soldiers but the scenes of its occupation. He moved later to Little Rock and continued his work. Bankes would stay on in Little Rock after the war where he would become what the *Arkansas Gazette* would later call the city's most prominent photographer. He remained through the 1870s, his studio listed in the city's business directory as late as 1878. Some time after this, he moved to Chicago where he lived for about twenty-five years. He returned to Arkansas, however, in 1906 where he died. Bankes was clearly the most ambitious of the state's photographers, mimicking in his later work the practices of Mathew Brady. His best known work would be the publishing in the early 1870s of his "Gallery of Famous Arkansans," modeled after Brady's 1850 "Gallery of Illustrious Americans."

Men such as White and Bankes, while leaving a photographic heritage hardly comparable to that of their contemporaries in the theaters of action east of the Mississippi River, nonetheless add to the visual impressions that we have of the American Civil War. All of these photographers left an image of the men who fought and the world of nineteenth century warfare. Brady said of his own work, "The camera is the eye of history." History's eye was also on the war in Arkansas, and the work of those pioneer photographers in the state show us something of what history saw.

Of all aspects of the Civil War in Arkansas, photography documents least well the operations of the various photographers themselves who worked in the state. The only set of photographs showing anything at all about these men consists of three images connected with the work of R. H. White. White was one of the most prolific of the wartime photographers. Many of the outdoor photographs that still remain appear to have been made by him. This self-portrait was made at Little Rock, probably after 1864. (*Photo courtesy of the Arkansas History Commission*)

White probably came to Arkansas from the Midwest with the Union army. His name first appears on *cartes de visite* made at De Valls Bluff after it was occupied by General Frederick Steele's army in 1863. At some point, White took the time to photograph his own shop in that town. His studio appears to be on the right, with a canvas roof. On the left is his office with examples of his work displayed on shelves around the windows. The individuals in the photograph are not identified, but possibly he managed to slip into his own picture, as his contemporary Mathew Brady often did, and he might very well be the individual looking out from the office. (*Photo courtesy of the Arkansas History Commission*)

White moved to Little Rock sometime in 1864. This photograph shows his shop on Markham. On the rear of the building can be seen a maneuverable skylight that allowed him to capture the best light from the north. This photograph was probably made in the spring of 1865 when White was documenting the construction that had taken place and the facilities taken over by the army for the United States government. (*Photo courtesy of the National Archives*)

Much of the photographic legacy of the Civil War in Arkansas remains in existence because of Orville Gillett of the Third Michigan Cavalry. In 1864, Gillett became a lieutenant in the Third Arkansas Cavalry and remained in Arkansas after the war. Gillett collected not only numerous individual portraits of the men who served with him, but also purchased many outdoor scenes done by R. H. White. Gillett's papers were later given to the Arkansas History Commission and contained these photographs. The scenes done outdoors, perhaps the best from the period, were pasted onto leaves of his diaries and, fortunately, preserved. (*Photo courtesy of the Arkansas History Commission*)

The only other documented photographer of outdoor scenes during the war was Thomas W. Bankes. Bankes worked at Helena during the war and captured Union activity there. In particular, he left a legacy of dozens of flood scenes made during the Mississippi River's frequent overflows. These two photographs by Bankes show a Helena home with contrabands in front, and the same house during the flood of 1864. (*Photos courtesy of the UALR Archives*)

About most of the other photographers, little is known, and few of their works survive. Much of what remains concerning their work and personal lives comes from the information that is provided on the backs of their photographs.

"GEM"
PHOTOGRAPH GALLERY,
Markham Street,
Opposite Head-Quarters,
LITTLE ROCK, ARK.

HENRY SLATTER, - - - Proprietor.

Pictures colored to life if desired. Duplicates can be had at any time within a year.

FROM
BROWN'S
GALLERY,
MAIN STREET,
Little Rock, Ark.

Chapter 1

Arkansas Goes to War

The election of Abraham Lincoln as President of the United States in November, 1860, started the states of the South towards secession, beginning with South Carolina the following December. Although the people of Arkansas were certainly citizens of a southern state, no early consensus developed in favor of secession. A population of 324,143 whites and 111,259 blacks, mostly slaves, lived in this frontier community of the Old South. While slavery was an integral part of their economy and society, too many advantages remained for staying in the Union to encourage quick action. A few prominent leaders pushed for secession, most noteworthy being United States Senator Robert Ward Johnson, Congressman Thomas C. Hindman, and the governor elected in 1860, Henry Massie Rector. Equally strong pro-Union support, however, came from individuals such as Senator William King Sebastian and William M. Fishback. Strong Unionist sentiments managed to delay secession through the spring of 1861 against vigorous agitation for leaving the Union.

The strongest supporter for secession in 1860 and 1861 turned out to be Governor Rector. In a special message to the legislature in December, 1860, Rector urged arming the militia and preparing for war. He also successfully secured the meeting of a state convention to consider withdrawing from the Union. Prior to the election for that convention, he precipitated a major crisis when he demanded the surrender of the United States Arsenal in Little Rock. Only the willingness of Captain James Totten to concede to the governor's demands on February 8, 1861, prevented bloodshed.

The convention that met at Little Rock on March 4, 1861, turned out in favor of the Unionists. David Walker of Washington County, who opposed secession, beat B. C. Totten of Prairie County for president of the convention by a vote of 40 to 35. The sessions of the convention were turbulent, and great hostility existed between the secession and anti-secession factions. Despite vigorous agitation for secession, the Unionist majority could not be swayed, and when the convention adjourned on March 21, one of its last acts was passage of a resolution that stated the people of Arkansas preferred to remain in the Union. The delegates agreed, however, to reconvene later if the situation should change.

The firing on Fort Sumter on April 12, 1861, changed the situation in the state. On April 15, President Lincoln asked for seventy-five thousand troops from the states to suppress lawless elements in the South. Governor Rector and others pressured David Walker, president of the convention, to reconvene that body, and Walker was unable to resist. When it met again at Little Rock on May 6, sentiment had changed to the point that secession could not be stopped. Even such prominent opponents of secession at the early session as Crawford County's Jesse Turner, railroad promoter and entrepreneur, had changed their minds. This time the vote for secession passed easily 65 to 5. When the president asked that the vote be made unanimous, only one, Isaac Murphy of Madison County, refused to sustain the majority.

The convention's action meant war, and a war fever quickly spread throughout the state. The convention itself appropriated $2,000,000 to arm state troops, established a war board, and authorized Governor Rector to call up thirty thousand men to meet the emergency. The convention adjourned on June 3; Rector and his board then called for ten thousand volunteers. Rector's "Army of Arkansas" was commanded by General James Yell, with N. Bart Pearce and N. B. Burrow as brigadier generals. Albert Pike was sent to the Indian Territory to secure the help of the Indians there known as the Civilized Tribes. Rector's army disappeared in the summer of 1861 as these state troops were taken over by the Confederate government.

The desire to fight was so intense that state authorities had to turn away many who wanted to join because of the lack of equipment and arms for them. Still, pro-Southern sympathizers formed local units across the state with names such as the "Tyronza Rebels," the "Hempstead Hornets," the "Montgomery Hunters," the "Muddy Bayou Heroes," the "Polk County Invincibles," and the "Camden Knights." As early as January, 1861, fifty-five young men from Crawford County formed the Van Buren Frontier Guards "for the purpose of instructing ourselves in the art of war and if necessary for domestic defense."[1] They also agreed to submit to the regulations of the group, and to meet promptly for drill at 7 p.m. on Monday, Wednesday, and Thursday. Absent members were fined twenty-five cents.

They came to camp believing that the war would be short and heroic. Sir Henry Morton Stanley, who joined the Sixth Arkansas Infantry in the summer of 1861, remembered his first days in camp:

The fever of military enthusiasm was at its height, in man, woman and child; and we, who were to represent them in the war, received far more adulation than was good for us. The popular praise turned our young heads giddy, and anyone who doubted that we were the sanest, bravest, and most gallant boys in the world, would have been in personal danger! Unlike the Spartans, there was not modesty in the estimate of our valour. After a few drills, we could not even go to draw rations without the practice of the martial step, and crying 'Guide centre,' or 'right wheel,' or some other order we had learned. At our messes, we talked of tactics, and discussed Beauregard's and Lee's merits, glorified Southern chivalry, and depreciated the Yankees, became fluent in the jargon of patriotism, and vehement in our hatred of the enemy.[2]

At the end of the summer these units were marching off to war amidst a carnival-like atmosphere. At Washington, Arkansas, John R. Gratiot, a veteran of the Mexican War and now a captain of the Hempstead Rifles, formed his company in front of the hotel where it received its flag from Miss Betty Conway. A large crowd watched as the young lady urged the eager soldiers to "go in the defense of liberty and independence."[3] Shortly after two o'clock in the afternoon, the band playing and the crowd cheering, the column marched out of town and off to the adventure all knew was soon to come.

By the end of the first year of war the state had enrolled 21,500 troops. During the entire course of the conflict the state furnished about 60,000 men to the Confederate cause, possibly even more. Although it is impossible to name the exact number of units, at least forty-six infantry regiments, seventeen cavalry regiments, and thirteen batteries of artillery had been organized. In addition, however, there were numerous state organizations that served, including the Arkansas battalion, composed of the old, the sick, and the young, that was enlisted in the spring of 1864 to stop a Federal invasion of southwestern sections.

State authorities from the beginning feared that the Confederate government intended to move the Arkansas regiments east of the Mississippi River. In fact, of those raised in the first year of the war, most were moved to the eastern battlefields. As a result, Arkansas was forced to defend its own territory with Missourians, Texans, Indians, and those troops that could be scraped up after the initial enlistments had taken the best of Arkansas' youth. Local officials had no choice, however, but to comply with Confederate demands. The removal of the state's troops was made possible when the military board authorized their transfer to Confederate service on July 15, 1861. Of the infantry regiments organized in Arkansas, only twelve units, about one fourth of those raised, served almost totally in the state. In addition, thirteen of the cavalry regiments and four of the artillery units saw service only within state confines.

The units that left Arkansas saw difficult service throughout the war. The first unit organized (the First Arkansas) was rushed to Virginia where it was on the field during the battle of First Bull Run, although not engaged. It then went on to fight at Shiloh. The Third Infantry was the only regiment to serve throughout the war in the eastern theater of operations. The Third fought with Lee's Army of Northern Virginia from Malvern Hill to Petersburg. It also appeared at Chickamauga when General Longstreet was detached to stop a Union invasion of northern Georgia. However, most troops served in the division of Arkansan Patrick Ronayne Cleburne in the Army of Tennessee. The Second, Fifth, Sixth, Seventh, and Eighth constituted the brigade of St. John R. Liddell. The First, Thirteenth, and Fifteenth were part of Lucius E. Polk's brigade. Under varying commanders and organizations, Arkansas troops in the west fought at Shiloh, Port Hudson, Perryville, Vicksburg, Murfreesboro, Chickamauga, Missionary Ridge, Atlanta, Franklin, Bentonville, and almost all the other engagements in this theater.

The realities of war proved to be less romantic than imagined for those who had first marched off. The individual soldier often spent more time in camp preparing for battle than fighting. When battle came it seldom produced heroes. Death or capture became the lot of many soldiers and death came, as often as not, from diseases rather than from an enemy's bullet. Measles and other maladies cursed the camps. While casualty figures are very inexact of troops from all states in the Confederacy, about nine percent died in battle or from wounds while sixteen percent succumbed to disease and accident.

As many as thirteen thousand Confederate soldiers may have spent some period of the war in Northern prisons. Those captured after 1863 probably returned only after the war had ended. The death of the dream produced an early reduction in volunteers. After the first year, the numbers responding to calls to join the flag declined to the point that authorities enacted conscription. After April 16, 1862, all white males from 18 to 35 were susceptible to service.

The lessons of war began at the end of the secession summer for the men of Arkansas. The late summer of 1861 brought the realities of war into the lives of almost everyone in the state. As an invading army led by Union General Nathaniel Lyon marched southward out of St. Louis towards their state, units of Governor Rector's Army of Arkansas marched to meet the invaders. On August 10, Arkansans would first encounter the enemy in Missouri at the battle of Wilson's Creek or Oak Hills. In a battle that would be one of the costliest of the war in terms of men engaged, these troops would have their mettle severely tested.

Henry M. Rector, elected governor in 1860, led the secession movement in Arkansas. Although he had run for office on a Unionist platform, the new governor, in his inaugural message on November 15, 1860, urged the state legislature to secede. Members of the legislature proved reluctant to act. Rector continued his agitation, and with support from other public officials he pressured the legislators. On December 21, he sent another special message in which he urged secession and military preparations. He informed the members, "The wisest and best government that has ever been allotted by man, has fallen prey to the madness and fanaticism of its own children, for I am convinced, that the Union of these States, in this moment is practically severed, and gone forever." Still the legislature delayed passing any secession measure. Not until January did it finally pass a bill, but that only directed the governor to call an election on February 18 to decide whether or not there should be a convention and also to elect delegates. With this minimal action, Rector proceded with his efforts to lead the state out of the Union. (*Photo courtesy of the UALR Archives*)

Governor Rector's position received strong support from members of the state's Congressional delegation. United States Senator Robert W. Johnson, patriarch of the political faction known as the "Family," had long believed that an end of the Union was inevitable. As a congressman in 1850, he had seen the compromise of that year as the first step towards Northern domination of the South. After 1853, as a United States senator, Johnson remained silent on the sectional issue in public, but concluded in private that at some point the Union would be dissolved. The election of Abraham Lincoln and the calling of a secession convention by South Carolina led the senator to issue a letter to the people of Arkansas on December 1, 1860, urging them to support the action of the South Carolinians. On December 21, he joined with Congressman Thomas C. Hindman in the first of two joint messages. The two pressed the state legislature to summon a state convention to lead Arkansas out of the Union along with South Carolina. In the events that took place during the spring of 1861, Johnson remained an ardent supporter of secession. (*Photo courtesy of the Arkansas History Commission*)

One of the most outspoken agitators for secession was Thomas C. Hindman, shown here when he served in the U.S. Congress. As a young man, he had been elected to the Mississippi General Assembly where, during the debate over the Compromise of 1850, he had openly supported the right of any state to secede. In 1854, Hindman moved to Helena, where he became involved in politics, and his hot temper often led him into violent confrontations. In 1854, for example, Hindman and his friend Patrick R. Cleburne became involved in a gunfight with several political opponents. One man died in the mêlée, Cleburne was badly wounded, and Hindman himself was shot. In 1858, Hindman was elected to the U.S. Congress, where he became one of the leading fire-eaters. During the secession crisis, he did everything in his power to dissolve the Union. If the South were invaded, he once said on the floor, "the price of hemp will go up, for our whole crop will be needed to hang the abolition soldiery."[4] On May 6, 1861, Hindman proudly telegraphed Jefferson Davis that the Arkansas Convention passed the "ordinance of secession at 4 p.m. by a unanimous vote." (*Photo courtesy of the Chicago Historical Society*)

The United States Arsenal at Little Rock was the scene of the first confrontation between state and federal authorities. Constructed in the 1840s to provide support for troops that might be used against Indians, during the 1850s the Arsenal was used to repair equipment and store munitions. In November, 1860, after years in which its sole occupants had been a storekeeper and a few non-commissioned officers and mechanics, the army transferred the Second United States Artillery to the facility. Captain James Totten and his seventy-five men had quietly occupied the arsenal, but rumors that the government intended to further reinforce Totten caused wide concern. The spread of this rumor in January, 1861, led a mass meeting at Helena to offer Governor Rector five hundred men to take

Arsenal Building

the Arsenal. Rector's subsequent actions suggest that he saw this offer as an opportunity to push the people towards secession and to influence the upcoming vote for a convention. Rector refused to accept troops, but telegraphed to Helena, "Should the people assemble in their defense, the governor will interpose his official position in their behalf."[5] This message was all that was needed to encourage nearly a thousand men to assemble at Little Rock and demand the removal of the Federal troops. Captain Totten defused a potentially explosive situation when he decided to abandon the Arsenal. Rector assumed control on February 7. Only Totten's action had prevented armed conflict. (*Photos courtesy of the UALR Archives*)

Enlisted men's barracks

Officers' quarters

Magazine

On February 18, 1861, Arkansans had voted in favor of a convention to consider the state's relationship to the Union. When it convened on March 4, 1861, however, Unionists were in control. David Walker from Washington County was the most important of the Unionist delegates. Walker had been a member of the state constitutional convention in 1836 and had served as a judge on the state supreme court. Walker had earlier written about the possibility of secession, "When I look at the blessings the Union has conferred on us, I feel like it would be almost sacrilege to even think of seeing it dissolved."[6] Now he had the opportunity to prevent secession. The Unionist majority elected him as president of the convention. The sessions of the convention were chaotic. The Unionists were taunted by their secessionist colleagues, the crowds in the galleries, and those outside who called for action. When secessionists introduced a resolution calling for immediate secession, Unionists defeated it by a vote of 35 to 39. Almost stalemated, the convention dragged on until March 21, when the delegates finally agreed to submit the issue of secession to the people the following August. Pledged to resist any coercion, they stated that they preferred a peaceful settlement of their problems within the Union. Walker and the Unionists behind him had stalled the drive towards secession. (*Photo courtesy of the UALR Archives*)

United States Senator William K. Sebastian became one of the strongest opponents to secession following the adjournment of the state convention in March, 1861. His opposition to secession incurred extreme hostility from the fire-eaters who were ready for disunion. When Arkansas seceded, Sebastian refused to resign from the United States Senate. While he did not attend a special session of Congress called by Lincoln in the summer of 1861 and was expelled, he refused to support the Confederacy and settled in Memphis during the war. When that city was captured by Union forces, Sebastian remained and swore allegiance to the government. On May 20, 1865, he died at Memphis. After the war he would be restored posthumously to his Senate seat, and his family was paid his salary as a senator from the time of his expulsion until his death. (*Photo courtesy of the UALR Archives*)

Following Fort Sumter and President Lincoln's call upon the state for troops to suppress secessionist forces, when David Walker was forced to reconvene the state convention, Unionist forces were no longer in control. Even Walker was unwilling to sustain the Union after Lincoln had called for troops and made clear his intention of preventing secession. One Unionist who refused to surrender his ideals, however, was Isaac Murphy. A native of Madison County, Murphy had served two years in the lower house of the General Assembly and one term in the state senate prior to the war. He was elected to the state convention in 1861 as a pro-Union delegate. In the reconvened convention, delegates adopted a secession ordinance by a vote of 65 to 55, on the first day of its meeting, May 6, 1861. David Walker, after the vote, told the delegates, "since we all must go, let us all go together."[7] He asked for a unanimous vote in favor of secession. Four of those who had stood against the ordinance changed their vote to "aye," but Murphy rose and announced that he could not conscientiously vote for secession. "I therefore vote 'no,'"[8] he said. From the gallery, Mrs. Frederick Trapnall threw him a bouquet. (*Photo courtesy of the UALR Archives*)

After passing its ordinance of secession, the state convention created a military board to supervise the war effort, appropriated two million dollars for the board's activities, and authorized the calling out of thirty thousand men for service. Under the convention's authorization, patriotic southerners organized military units throughout Arkansas in the spring and summer of 1861. Among those units was the Third Arkansas Infantry Volunteers organized in June, 1861. Company H of that unit drew heavily upon the young men of Clark County for its members. Required to provide their own uniforms and usually bringing their own weapons, these young men mustered at Arkadelphia in preparation for joining their regiment at Little Rock. The Third would retain its identity through the battle of Wilson's Creek, where it suffered heavy casualties in the defense of Woodruff's battery against a Federal assault. The unit's commander, Colonel John R. Gratiot, reported, ". . . they maintained their position thirty minutes under one of the most galling fires ever delivered upon a regiment."[9] One hundred thirteen of the regiment's members were killed or wounded. After Wilson's Creek, the regiment was disbanded and its members integrated into other Confederate units. (*Photo courtesy of Henderson State Museum*)

Van H. Manning, shown here with his wife, Mary, was called an impetuous Southerner by Confederate historian John M. Harrell. He helped organize two companies at his hometown of Hamburg in Ashley County at the beginning of the war, then marched them to Vicksburg only to have the Confederate secretary of war refuse their service. Undeterred, Manning marched his men to Lynchburg, Virginia, where, joined by other recruits from southeast Arkansas, they were to become the well-known Third Arkansas Infantry. Manning's unit was the only Arkansas regiment to serve in the Virginia theater throughout the war, participating in every major battle. Originally the major of the regiment, on March 11, 1862, Manning was promoted to colonel. Manning served as an exemplary commander. On October 17, 1863, General James Longstreet recommended him for promotion to brigadier general, noting that the colonel "enjoys the reputation of being one of the most active and capable officers of his rank in the service."[10] The lack of vacancies, however, prevented his promotion. On May 6, 1864, Manning was shot in his right thigh in the Battle of the Wilderness and captured. The colonel recovered but was sent first to Morris Island, where a friend reported that he was in destitute condition and asked for his pay from the Confederate government. He was later sent to Capitol Prison, then to Fort Delaware, to Hilton Head in South Carolina, then back to Fort Delaware. While he swore an oath of allegiance to the United States government in December, 1864, Manning remained in Federal prisons until released by a presidential order on July 21, 1865. (*Photo courtesy of Pamela Manning Fein*)

Richard Jesse Bailey enlisted in Company H, Third Arkansas Infantry for the "duration" on March 17, 1862. Bailey, a Virginian whose motives for joining the Arkansas unit are not clear, was assigned to the staff as a member of the band a month after his enlistment. Bailey served with his unit in all of its major battles afterward. He was one of the few who survived battles at Antietam, Gettysburg, Chickamauga, the Wilderness, and Spotsylvania. On the list of those men who surrendered with Lee at Appomattox, he was one of only seven men left of his original company. (*Photo courtesy of the Arkansas History Commission*)

While the Third Arkansas went to Virginia, most of the units organized in the summer of 1861 would wind up in the Army of Mississippi as General Albert Sidney Johnston concentrated Confederate troops in southwestern Kentucky to resist an invasion by Federal forces. Many of these units would see continued service in the division of Brigadier General William J. Hardee, shown here, and then of Patrick Cleburne. In July, Hardee received seven infantry regiments, one cavalry regiment and a cavalry battalion, and units of artillery into Confederate service. Originally intending to operate in Missouri, Hardee moved the command to Kentucky upon the orders of Major General Leonidas Polk, who concluded that the defense of Arkansas would be conducted better east of the Mississippi River. (*Photo courtesy of Greg McMahon*)

Colonel David C. Cross, a wealthy land speculator who lived in what is now Cross County, organized the Fifth Arkansas Infantry, one of the units to cross the Mississippi with Hardee. The Fifth went to Columbus, Kentucky, then participated in the fall back to Corinth, Mississippi, after Confederate defeats at forts Henry and Donelson had made their position along the Mississippi River undefendable. While in Kentucky, Cross contracted pneumonia and never completely recovered. The Fifth went on to distinguish itself in battles at Corinth, Stone's River, Chickamauga, Atlanta, Franklin, Nashville, and finally surrendered with Joseph Johnston in North Carolina. Cross, however, received a medical discharge on May 12, 1862, and returned to Arkansas. In this picture, Cross, on the right, is with Lieutenant Willis P. Wilkins who lived near him. Wilkins joined J. H. McGehee's regiment of Arkansas cavalry and saw service with that unit in Arkansas throughout the war. (*Photo courtesy of the Arkansas History Commission*)

John Gould Fletcher was a member of the
Capitol Guards, mustered into Confederate
service as Company A of the Sixth Arkansas Infantry on June 10, 1861. As part of
Hardee's Corps at Shiloh, the Sixth was in
the front of the attack and suffered badly,
although only four men were killed. One of
the wounded was the commander of Company A, Captain Gordon Peay, and in elec-
tions at Corinth, Mississippi, the unit
elected Fletcher as its new captain. In June,
1862, the regiment moved to Chattanooga
and was involved in fighting in Tennessee
and Kentucky through the fall of that year.
On December 31, the Sixth, now consolidated with the Seventh Regiment, took part
in the Battle of Murfreesboro. During the
battle, Fletcher was severely wounded and
abandoned on the battlefield. After spending a freezing night, he was carried to the
home of the McFadden family of Murfreesboro where he recovered. Imprisoned for
nearly a year, Fletcher rejoined his unit in
December, 1863, in Georgia. For him, however, the battle was over. Unable to serve in
the field, he was assigned to a court martial
board in Atlanta and remained in that service through the rest of the war. (*Photo
courtesy of the UALR Archives*)

William Shores was another Arkansan who joined the Confederate service in 1861 and was moved from the state. Only seventeen years old, Shores joined "The City Guards" at Camden on July 26, 1861. The "Guards" became Company H of the Sixth Arkansas Regiment. Shores was appointed drummer on December 4, 1861, and perhaps marched with his unit at Shiloh on April 6 and 7, 1862. Shortly after the battle, Shores was hospitalized at Holly Springs, Mississippi, then furloughed home during the summer. He rejoined his regiment sometime in the autumn of 1862 and was with it at the battle of Murfreesboro where he was shot in the stomach. The young drummer was taken to the Fair Ground's Hospital in Atlanta. Given the medical technology of the day, little could be done, and Shores died on January 7, 1863. Not the first to die in the Sixth, Shores would not be the last. His regiment continued through the war in Tennessee and Georgia, suffering terrible casualties at Chickamauga, Missionary Ridge, and Franklin. (*Photo courtesy of the Museum of the Confederacy*)

William A. Halliburton was a member of
the Seventh Arkansas Infantry, another
unit that was part of the Arkansas Brigade
in Hardee's Corps. A farmer from Stone
County, Halliburton joined his unit at
Camp Shaver near Pocahontas in Randolph
County. The unit went to Kentucky with
Hardee and took part in the retreat from
that state in 1861. On April 6 and 7, 1862, it
was in the midst of the heaviest action at
Shiloh. Losses in that battle caused General
Hardee to call the unit "the bloody Seventh." Following the battle, only one hundred members of the regiment were able to
march from the field. Halliburton survived
Shiloh, and was with the unit at
Murfreesboro the following December
when it fought in combination with the Sixth
Regiment. Halliburton was shot in the knee
in the battle, but was able to retreat with his
regiment. His service continued until September 1, 1864, when he was captured near
Jonesboro, Georgia. He was exchanged on
September 19 and fought on with the regiment until its surrender. (*Photo courtesy of
Mike Polston*)

The First Arkansas Infantry, or Fagan's
Regiment, joined the Army of Mississippi
in March, 1862. This unit had been the first
to respond to the call for volunteers and
had been organized in May, 1861. Captain
Charles S. Stark, a farmer from Arkadelphia, was typical of its members. Stark put
together the Clark County Volunteers
which would become Company B of the
First Infantry. At the request of Confederate
officials at Richmond, the First was sent to
Virginia to aid in the defense of the capital.
While in reserve at the first battle of Bull
Run, the First saw no action. Stark's experiences were like those of many other new
soldiers. He became sick in Virginia and
was hospitalized at Fredericksburg through
the winter of 1861–1862. He returned to
his unit when it moved to Tennessee, however, and Stark was with his company on
April 6, 1862, when it staged a bloody bayonet assault at the "Hornet's Nest." That
day the First Arkansas lost thirty percent of
its men killed and wounded. The following
July, Stark resigned his commission and left
the service. The reason is not known. He
apparently never returned to Arkansas.
(*Photo courtesy of David Perdue*)

John M. W. Baird, eighteen, and Henry Clements, both of Jacksonport, joined the Jacksonport Guards in the first rush to the flag. As Company G of the First Arkansas Infantry, members of the Jacksonport unit were involved in all of the unit's major engagements—Shiloh, Perryville, Murfreesboro, Chickamauga, Missionary Ridge, Atlanta, Franklin, Nashville, and then the surrender at Greensboro. Baird's service was undistinguished. He was promoted to corporal, then reduced to the ranks in August, 1863, for losing his haversack. Clements enlisted as third corporal and rose to first sergeant. Clements was captured at Jonesboro, Georgia, September 1, 1864, then exchanged later that month. On November 30, 1864, Clements was wounded at the battle of Franklin but remained with his unit. He fought on to the end, surrendering with his unit at Milledgeville, Georgia, on May 4, 1865. (*Photo courtesy of the Arkansas History Commission*)

Christopher C. Scott, a twenty-two-year-old clerk, and Christopher Thrower, a twenty-three-year-old lawyer, joined the Camden Knights in May, 1861, in their home town. Led by Captain William L. Crenshaw, the Knights marched to Pine Bluff and then took a steamer to Little Rock where they joined the First Arkansas Infantry. Thrower served with the unit through all its major battles until the end of the war. Scott served with the unit through the siege at Corinth, then returned to Camden where he helped to organize the Appeal Battery. Scott rose to the rank of captain with the battery, was captured with his unit at Vicksburg, then served in the Trans-Mississippi after his parole. (*Photo courtesy of the Museum of the Confederacy*)

Henry A. Hill was another of the many young men who joined the Camden Knights in Ouachita County in May, 1861. Hill was born in Arkansas, but his parents were from Massachusetts. The elder Hill had settled in the prospering Ouachita River town of Camden as a merchant. Henry, or Harry, served with the unit through all of its early engagements. On January 24, 1862, he re-enlisted for a two-year period and received a bounty of fifty dollars. Hill's luck ended in the trenches around Atlanta when General John Hood hurled Cleburne's division against the Federal left to prevent General Sherman from encircling the city from the east. While it delayed Sherman's triumph, little else was accomplished. Hill was listed as absent from his unit after the battle on July 22, 1864. Apparently wounded in the fray, Hill died from his wounds. (*Photo courtesy of the Museum of the Confederacy*)

For the units that went east, but were not attached to Hardee's corps, service often involved garrisoning Confederate positions along the Mississippi River. Such duty often proved disastrous. William F. Morton enlisted as a private in the Eleventh Arkansas Infantry at Pine Bluff in August, 1861. He marched with his unit to New Madrid, Missouri, where he spent the winter of 1861–1862. That spring the unit was engaged in the battle to protect New Madrid and Island No. 10. When Federal forces besieged the fortifications at Island No. 10 on March 15, the Eleventh and Morton were caught. During the siege Morton was wounded, the ball that hit him reputedly damaging the daguerrotype from which the copy of his photo was made. When the Confederates surrendered at Island No. 10 on April 8, 1862, Morton was hospitalized aboard the United States hospital ship *Empress*. With the other men he was then sent to Camp Douglas, Illinois, until exchanged the following November. Afterwards Morton would join the Eleventh and Seventeenth Consolidated Mounted Infantry and serve with this unit in Mississippi through the rest of the war. (*Photo courtesy of Mike Polston*)

George W. Elliott of Camden had wanted as a boy to be a soldier. His parents sent him to Nashville, Tennessee, to a military academy. Before graduation, however, he returned to his hometown where he joined Company G of the Eleventh Arkansas Infantry. This second unit of "Camden Knights" that went to war had the misfortune to be at Island No. 10. With the other prisoners, Elliott was sent to Camp Douglas near Chicago. For Elliott the prison camp with its overcrowding and poor protection from the cold was fatal. He contracted pneumonia and died on May 3, 1862. A friend remembered him as he had been before the war, writing "I fancy I can see him yet, with his brown eyes, auburn curls and smiling face. He was his mother's youngest child and she loved him with a tender and beautiful devotion." (*Photo courtesy of the Museum of the Confederacy*)

Vicksburg, which surrendered on July 4, 1863, was another trap for Confederate Arkansans. Joseph Vital Bogy of Pine Bluff joined J. Y. Gains' battery at Little Rock in November, 1861. The battery was in northwest Arkansas in the spring of 1862, although it did not fight at Pea Ridge. Afterwards the battery moved to Memphis and was sent to Shiloh, but arrived too late for the battle. They finally saw battle at Hatchie Bridge on October 5, 1862, as they helped clear and hold the pontoon bridge across the Hatchie River until Confederate forces retreating from an attack on Corinth could pass. Assigned next to Vicksburg, Bogy's battery was surrendered and sent to a parole camp at Demopolis, Alabama. At the time of the surrender, Bogy reported that of the twenty-six men who had gone into the lines at Vicksburg, thirteen were killed and wounded, and both of the battery's guns had been destroyed. After being paroled, Bogy joined the Second Missouri Battery and served with the armies of Johnston and Hood until surrendering in Alabama at the end of the war. (*Photo courtesy of the Arkansas History Commission*)

38

Francis Warford enlisted in Company E of the Nineteenth Arkansas Infantry in Hot Spring County on March 1, 1862. His enlistment was for one year. The Nineteenth or Dockery's regiment performed as engineers around Little Rock in the spring of 1862. That autumn they were transferred to General Sterling Price's Army of the West in Mississippi and ordered to hold the line there while Braxton Bragg drove into Tennessee from Tupelo, Mississippi. The Nineteenth was heavily engaged in the battle at Corinth on October 3 and 4, 1862, and in later skirmishes attempting to prevent Grant from seizing Vicksburg. With other units, the Nineteenth and Francis Warford pulled back into Vicksburg and were besieged. Warford and the unit surrendered on July 4, Warford signing his parole papers with an X. What happened to Warford after the surrender is not clear, but he appears not to have served further. (*Photo courtesy of the Old Washington State Park*)

Hundreds more Arkansans fell into Federal hands when Confederate forces surrendered the garrison at Port Hudson on July 8, 1863. Major Elisha H. Messick of the Fourteenth Arkansas Infantry had left his job as a saddler in Marion County in the fall of 1861 to join the Fourteenth at Fort Smith. The unit saw action at Pea Ridge, Corinth, Iuka, and against Grant around Vicksburg. Captured at Port Hudson, Messick was sent north on the steamer *Planet* and imprisoned at the Federal prison at Rock Island, Illinois. As an officer he was not eligible for parole and would spend the rest of the war in that prison. (*Photo courtesy of the Arkansas History Commission*)

For the Arkansas troops at Port Hudson, the suffering was as bad as for those at Vicksburg. On May 23, the Confederate garrison there had been surrounded by an overwhelming Union force under General Nathaniel Banks. Banks threw his men against the trenches at Port Hudson on May 27 and June 14 and was repulsed both times. After the second attack, he decided to starve out the garrison. In the garrison was the Fifteenth Arkansas Infantry with an artillery battery attached. After a month of siege, the fort had no more food and the men resorted to eating whatever was available. After Vicksburg's surrender on July 4, the situation at Port Hudson was hopeless and the Confederate command was surrendered there on July 8. All that was left in the area was devastation, as is shown by these photographs of the gun emplacement of the battery of the Fifteenth Arkansas. (*Photos courtesy of the UALR Archives*)

P. Lynch Lee was a native of Alabama who had moved to Camden in 1859. Like many other young men, Lee joined the Camden Knights, which was to be a unit of the First Arkansas Infantry in May, 1861. Illness prevented his departure with that unit, so he remained at home until he had the opportunity of joining the Fifteenth Arkansas Infantry later that summer. The men of the regiment elected Lee its major. Along with the Sixth, Seventh, and Twelfth Regiments, Major Lee and the Fifteenth were rushed to Tennessee to help defend forts Henry and Donelson and prevent Federal movements up the Cumberland and Tennessee rivers. Lee was captured when Fort Henry fell on February 6, 1862. He was imprisoned at Fort Warren in Massachusetts until exchanged in the autumn, 1862. Lee returned to Arkansas and rejoined the reorganized regiment, now under Colonel Benjamin W. Johnson, as it moved into Port Hudson. In the battle for that post on July 9, 1863, Lee was wounded and again captured with his unit. This time the war was over for Lee, who was moved to New Orleans, then to a prison camp at Johnson's Island where he remained until the end of the war. (*Photo courtesy of the Camden and Ouachita County Public Library of Arkansas*)

John J. Thomas, a planter, joined the Hempstead Rifles early in the war and was mustered into Company H of Griffith's Seventeenth Arkansas Infantry on April 13, 1862. Thomas saw little service before being sent to Mississippi and assigned with his company to construct fortifications at Port Hudson. Thomas was promoted to captain at Port Hudson. Caught in the Federal drive along the Mississippi in the summer of 1863, Thomas and his unit were captured. As an officer Thomas was sent to the Northern prison and remained there through the rest of the war. (*Photo courtesy of the South Arkansas Regional Archives*)

James M. May, shown without a beard, served with the Twenty-third Arkansas Infantry. The Twenty-third also was captured at Port Hudson in July, 1863. The son of a planter at Hollywood in Clark County, James May was only eighteen years old when he enlisted in March, 1862. He fought with his unit at Corinth and Hatchie Bridge, but then had the misfortune to be at Port Hudson. He was paroled after three days and apparently returned to military service. The Twenty-third was mounted and reorganized in the fall of 1863 and fought in the Trans-Mississippi until it surrendered at Marshall, Texas, in 1865. Shown with James in the picture is his older brother, George, who had enrolled in the Second Regiment of Arkansas Mounted Rifles in 1861 and fought at Corinth, Stone's River, Chickamauga, and Missionary Ridge. George disappeared in the fighting around Chattanooga, the company muster roll listing him as a deserter. Whether he deserted or was killed, George never returned to his home after the war. (*Photo courtesy of the South Arkansas Regional Archives*)

For most Arkansans, the Civil War turned out to be anything but heroic. It involved suffering and deprivation. The military career of William Buford Word typifies that of many. Word enlisted in Company H of the Twentieth Arkansas Infantry at Warren, Arkansas on February 28, 1862. He was thirty-nine years old, older than most. Word became ill at Warren, but recovered enough after two months' hospitalization at Memphis to return to his unit in northern Mississippi. He fought at Iuka on September 19, 1862, and at Corinth. At Corinth his company lost eight men, and he was wounded in his arm. Furloughed for forty-five days, he returned to his unit on November 20 and fought at Coffeeville, Mississippi, on December 5, 1862. That spring he applied for dismissal from the army. He left on March 31, 1863—the reason for leaving, old age. (*Photo courtesy of Mrs. Frank J. Wilson*)

Chapter 2

War in Northwest Arkansas

When the Civil War began, the overriding strategic issue in the Trans-Mississippi West was who would gain control of Missouri, and Arkansas' future was largely tied to the fate of its northern neighbor. Until the Union forces could pacify southern Missouri, there could be no question of invading Arkansas. In the spring of 1861, the pro-Southern minority, led by Governor Claiborne Jackson, had seized control of much of southern Missouri, and members of the secessionist-minded State Guard were confident enough to boldly encamp in the outskirts of St. Louis. Rumor had it that the Guard planned to seize the United States arsenal, and the discovery that arms were being shipped to the camp confirmed the worst fears of the fiery abolitionist arsenal commander, Nathaniel Lyon. Lyon was determined to act, and on May 10, 1861, he led a column of troops to the camp and demanded the surrender of the Missouri State Guard.

Lyon lost no time in following up on his victory. On June 15, he occupied the capital, Jefferson City, and two days later Lyon's troops routed the Missouri State Guard at Booneville. These bold actions did much to demoralize the pro-Confederate elements in Missouri, and by summer, secessionist influence had largely been reduced to the Southwest corner of the state. There, Confederate Brigadier General Ben McCulloch, leading 4,500 Arkansas and Louisiana troops, joined Major General Sterling Price's Missouri State Guardsmen. Together they numbered about ten thousand men and even though they had no tents, supplies, or uniforms, and little military training, the Confederates decided to take the offensive. On August 9, 1861, the Confederate army encamped near Wilson's Creek amid undergrowth of scraggly oaks in the rolling hills southwest of Springfield. The next morning Lyon's little army of 5,400 men moved out to attack.

Wilson's Creek was a minor engagement when compared to the decisive battles that were later fought east of the Mississippi River, but it was one of the most fiercely contested conflicts of the Civil War. All morning in the August heat these untrained soldiers slugged away at each other. Finally, Confederate numbers and the death of General Lyon forced the Union army to withdraw. They suffered over twelve hundred casualties, while inflicting almost that many losses on their adversaries. The victory at Wilson's Creek gave the Confederates a fleeting chance to regain what they had lost in the previous ten weeks, but the South was unable to capitalize on the opportunity. Immediately after the battle, Generals Price and McCulloch began bickering with each other about the proper strategy to follow. Price wanted to advance immediately to the Missouri River, but McCulloch demurred, arguing that not only was his army ill-equipped for such a move, but his orders were to protect Arkansas and the Indian Territory, and he could not do that from central Missouri. To make matters worse, most of the Arkansas troops under the command of General N. B. Pearce were in the service of the state, and their one-year term of enlistment was about to expire. The Arkansas troops had been reluctant to leave Arkansas in the first place since most felt that their sole duty was to protect their state. Despite urgings by Pearce and Colonel Thomas Hindman to transfer to the Confederate army, the troops voted overwhelmingly to remain in the state service. This meant that most were discharged by September 1, and McCulloch lost about one-third of his soldiers. Any chance of salvaging a strategic victory ended with the imminent loss of Pearce's troops, and with McCulloch's decision to withdraw back to northern Arkansas. By September 2, McCulloch's forces, minus all but twenty of the three thousand Arkansas state troops, were back across the border.

By the end of 1861, the Union army had regained the initiative that it had lost at Wilson's Creek, and under its new commander, General Samuel Ryan Curtis, the Army of the Southwest marched into northwest Arkansas. Meanwhile, Price and McCulloch's forces had withdrawn into the security of the Boston Mountains.

On March 2, 1862, General Earl Van Dorn, who had earlier been appointed overall commander in Arkansas, arrived to take personal command over his still bickering generals. He decided to advance immediately, and on March 4 the entire column of sixteen thousand men began winding its way out of the Boston Mountains. It was bitterly cold, and snow fell on the troops as they moved northward. On March 6, 1862, the two armies finally met in the shadows of a steep, scrub-oak-covered peak known as Pea Ridge. For two days the troops battled away, inflicting more than twenty-one hundred casualties on each other. Among the dead were Confederate Generals Ben McCulloch and James McIntosh. After taking a severe pummeling by the Union soldiers and now running low on ammunition, Van Dorn finally broke off the attack to begin his long painful retreat southward toward the Arkansas River. Along the march, the rainy cold weather and lack of food further demoralized the already disorganized soldiers. One soldier from the Third Louisiana remembered the men eating anything they could find—raw corn, potatoes, and turnips. At Van Winkle's mills, these same famished soldiers found a slop-barrel and "scrambled for the decayed contents like a drove of hogs."[1] Eventually the army straggled into Van Buren. Given time, the men would regain their confidence, but for now Van Dorn's force posed no immediate threat to anyone.

However, the Union army itself had also been badly mauled and was in no condition to pursue the disorganized Confederates. It had been a terrible fight. After seeing the battlefield, General Curtis sat down and wrote his brother telling him: "The scene is silent and sad. The vulture and the wolf now have the dominion and dead friends and foes sleep in the same lonely graves."[2] Shortly after the battle, Curtis moved most of his command northward toward his base at Rolla, Missouri. There his battered troops

46

could recover in safety and he could make plans for the future invasion of Arkansas.

Throughout the summer, smaller forces of Confederate and Union troops continued to maneuver and fight in northwest Arkansas and southwest Missouri, but the main efforts of both antagonists had shifted eastward as they battled for control of the strategic Mississippi River. Still, the Confederates hoped to recover their losses in the area. In the fall of 1862, General Thomas C. Hindman, now in command of all the Confederate forces in northwest Arkansas, concocted a wild scheme to attack Springfield, Missouri, and establish winter quarters in the area. Such a plan was clearly beyond the resources that Hindman had at his disposal, but he was undeterred. By December, Hindman had assembled about ten thousand troops at Van Buren, and even though many of the men lacked shoes, uniforms, and arms, he decided to advance anyway.

On December 7, Hindman's army stood on the defensive at Prairie Grove and fought off several attacks by Union forces under Generals James E. Blunt and Francis J. Herron. That evening Hindman withdrew southward. Like Wilson's Creek, Prairie Grove had been a small battle, but it too had been a mean fight. Out of a total of twenty thousand combatants, twenty-five hundred men were lost. By statistics, both armies were still almost equal, but the advantage clearly lay with the North. Hindman's army began to disintegrate as sickness and desertions took their toll. Large numbers of deserters began to arrive at Blunt's army, "declaring that they had been forced into the rebel army against their will, and wished now to return to their homes . . . they also stated that a large portion of Hindman's army were conscripts . . . who would leave him on the first favorable opportunity."[3]

On December 28, 1862, Hindman received word that Blunt was advancing toward him again, and the Confederate commander decided to withdraw from the area. In his haste, Hindman abandoned many desperately needed supplies and left behind four thousand sick and wounded soldiers. The remaining troops straggled toward Little Rock through freezing rain and snow, abandoning anything which slowed down their progress. Many were barefooted, none had tents, and few possessed blankets. In the middle of January, Hindman's army of five thousand "emaciated, frozen, and exhausted" men finally reached Little Rock.[4]

The campaign for northwest Arkansas was over, and the Confederacy would never again mount a serious invasion threat. Yet the Union victories at Pea Ridge and Prairie Grove did not give the Federals a secure staging area to occupy the rest of Arkansas. Clearly the Union army could not adequately supply its forces for a sustained period south of the Boston Mountains by relying on a tenuous communications line that ran back to the railhead at Rolla, Missouri. Northwest Arkansas had become a strategic dead end, and until the North could gain control of the Mississippi River and its tributaries, the rest of the state would be relatively safe from invasion. After 1862, neither side was willing to spend the resources needed to methodically control northwest Arkansas, and the war in that area degenerated into a vicious guerilla fight which gave quarter neither to soldier nor civilian.

The largest military outpost in western Arkansas was the Fort Smith Garrison. During the early months of the war, Confederate strategists believed that the Union army could not penetrate the Mississippi River Valley, and that consequently they would resort to strategic flanking attacks along the Confederacy's western border. Therefore, Confederate authorities viewed Fort Smith as an essential bastion to both protect the western border and to maintain contact with the South's new allies in the Indian Territory. The ample barracks and storage facilities at the garrison also made Fort Smith an ideal Confederate staging base for the campaigns at Pea Ridge and Prairie

Fort Smith Garrison in 1865. Showing from left to right: enlisted barracks, two officers' barracks, and the quartermaster's storehouse. (*Photo courtesy of the J. N. Heiskell Historical Collection, UALR Archives*)

Grove. The battles at Wilson's Creek and Pea Ridge seemed to confirm the Confederate belief that Arkansas would be invaded from the west, but by late 1862, it had become clear to both sides that control of Arkansas would be determined in the Mississippi Valley rather than in the west. When that strategic shift became apparent, Fort Smith's importance quickly declined. In 1863, Union forces finally occupied Fort Smith, and it became the western anchor of their defense along the Arkansas River. Throughout the remainder of the war, troops operating out of Fort Smith worked to subdue the rampant guerilla activities in the region.

Officers' Quarters, 1865. (*Photo courtesy of the Cravens Collection, UALR Archives*)

Enlisted barracks, 1865. (*Photo courtesy of the
Cravens Collection, UALR Archives*)

Indian Council House, 1865. (*Photo courtesy
of the Illinois State Historical Society*)

Even though northwest Arkansas did not prove to be a practical springboard for the occupation of the rest of the state, it did become an important recruiting area for the Federals. There, pro-Union sentiment was high and many Arkansans did join the army. Before the war ended, 8,289 Arkansans had enlisted to fight against the Confederacy. The majority of these men served in cavalry regiments, and since they were familiar with both the geography and the people, they were particularly effective against the guerillas that infested Arkansas. Over seventeen hundred would die in the service. The First Light Artillery Battery was the only Union artillery unit raised in Arkansas. It entered service on August 31, 1863, and later participated in General Frederick Steele's Camden expedition. During that campaign, it saw action at Prairie d'Ane, Poison Spring, and Jenkins' Ferry. When the battery mustered out on August 10, 1864, twenty-five of the original members had died in the service. This photograph was taken shortly after the unit mustered in at Fayetteville. (*Photo courtesy of the Washington County Historical Society*)

Sterling Price, like the majority of generals during the Civil War, had no previous formal military training. Prior to 1861, he had served three terms in the U.S. Congress and four years as governor. His only military experience was during the Mexican War when he commanded the Second Missouri Infantry, an outfit that saw only limited service in the conflict. During the secession crisis, Price, like most Missourians, favored remaining in the Union, but events forced most men to take sides. Price chose the South and was immediately appointed commander of the Missouri State Guard. "Old Pap," as his men affectionately called him, was personally brave, but he "was a strong-minded individualist, possessed of his own concept of fighting the war," and "pursuing his own policy whatever the effects on the total situation."[5] Under him were seven thousand armed Missourians, and Price was anxious to drive the Union army out of Missouri, but he could not take the offensive without the help of an equally pig-headed officer, Brigadier General Benjamin McCulloch. . . . (*Photo courtesy of the Arkansas History Commission*)

General Ben McCulloch surely had one of the most varied careers of any officer who served with the Confederacy in the Trans-Mississippi West. As a young man, he left his native Tennessee to join the Texans in their rebellion against Mexico. He arrived in time to participate in the battle of San Jacinto where Texas won its independence. McCulloch decided to remain in Texas, where he was a surveyor and Indian fighter. During the Mexican War, he served with distinction as a scout for General Zachary Taylor. When gold was discovered in California, he became a "forty-niner" but, like most of the adventurers, he failed to find a strike. McCulloch returned to Texas and then served six years as a United States marshal. During the secession crisis he was appointed colonel of the Texas State Troops and accepted the surrender of General Twigg's garrison in San Antonio. When the Civil War began he was commissioned a brigadier general in the Confederate army, and on May 11, 1861, he became commander of the Arkansas District. McCulloch had at his disposal about thirty-two hundred troops from Arkansas, Texas, and Louisiana. These well-armed and uniformed troops had enlisted in the Provisional Confederate Army for three years. Nearby, Brigadier General N. B. Pearce commanded another twenty-two hundred troops. Most of these men had volunteered only to protect Arkansas from invasion. Legally, Pearce answered to state authorities, but he consented to act in conjunction with General McCulloch's forces. McCulloch had a low opinion of the fighting qualities of Price's Missourians, but he yielded to Price's incessant demands for reinforcements and agreed to march into Missouri. After some bickering between the two men, Price agreed to subordinate himself to McCulloch's orders, but not before he loftily informed the Texan that he had "commanded in more battles than you ever saw."[6] On the night of August 9, the Confederate army of ten thousand was encamped a few miles southvance the next morning, but their opponent, Brigadier General Nathaniel Lyon, would move before they did. (*Photo courtesy of Mike Polston*)

No man did more to save Missouri for the Union than the young, impetuous Nathaniel Lyon. After graduating from West Point in 1841, he had fought in the Seminole Campaign and the Mexican War. In the 1850s he served in "Bleeding Kansas," and at the outbreak of the war Lyon was stationed in Fort Riley, Kansas. Lyon, with the reputation of harsh disciplinarian, was disliked by his men, but he was a staunch Unionist, and he had attracted the attention of another Unionist, Republican congressman Frank Blair of Missouri. Blair knew that if Missouri was to remain in the Union, it needed uncompromising soldiers like Lyon, and he used his influence to get him transferred to Missouri. Within ten weeks, Lyon's forces had shattered much of the pro-Confederate power in Missouri.

After his earlier victories, Lyon wanted to pursue the fleeing Confederates, but his superior, General John C. Fremont, had consistently ignored his pleas for reinforcements. In a fit of pique, Lyon declared that Fremont "is a worse enemy to me and the Union cause than Price and McCulloch and the whole damned tribe of rebels."[7] On August 9, Lyon decided to throw his little force of fifty-four hundred men against the rebels. He would lead the main attack from the north, while a much smaller column would attack from the south. That evening the two columns bivouacked a short distance from the sleeping Confederates. (*Photo courtesy of the UALR Archives*)

"I fights mit Sigel" was the boast of thousands of German-Americans who joined the army to serve with their idol, Franz Sigel. The German emigré, after fighting in the revolutions of 1848, had fled to America and eventually settled in St. Louis where he became an influential leader in the German community. Lyon had assigned Colonel Sigel command of the column that would attack from the south. The initial assault went well, but the Confederate resistance soon stiffened. By 11 A.M., Sigel himself had been routed and the Confederates could now concentrate their entire strength on Lyon's column. (*Photo courtesy of Greg McMahon*)

Among the troops in Lyon's column were two companies of the Second Missouri Volunteers, led by German-born Major Peter J. Osterhaus. As a young man, Osterhaus had been embroiled in the revolutions which erupted in Europe in 1848, and he, like many other Germans, later fled to America. Osterhaus was living in St. Louis when the war began, and he had raised his men largely from German immigrants. That morning, Osterhaus' 150 men anchored the right flank of Lyon's column. During the fighting, Osterhaus' soldiers were roughly handled by his fellow Missourians as they helped repel repeated Southern attacks on what became known as Bloody Hill. When Osterhaus finally withdrew with the retreating Federal army he left behind fifteen dead and forty more men wounded. On August 13, 1861, General Fremont acknowledged Osterhaus for his "gallant and meritorious" service. Seven months later he would again fight many of the same Southerners at Pea Ridge. (*Photo courtesy of the Missouri Historical Society*)

The night before the battle, Lieutenant Omer Weaver, shown in this photograph, camped near the Wire Road with the rest of his battery of state troops. In 1860, William E. Woodruff, Jr., the son of the founder of the *Arkansas Gazette,* had organized the battery and named it in honor of Dr. William Totten, a prominent doctor who was a favorite with every Little Rock child raised in Little Rock since 1839. His son, artillery Captain James Totten, U.S.A., commanded the Federal Arsenal in Little Rock. On February 8, 1861, a rag-tag militia force, which included the Totten Battery, accepted Captain Totten's surrender. Totten's disarmed men eventually boarded a steamer for St. Louis, but before the captain left, the citizens of Little Rock gave him a fine ceremonial sword. Six months later, Woodruff's battery, now renamed the Pulaski Light Battery, would again face Captain Totten, but this time he would be in command of the Second U.S. Artillery. On the morning of August 10, Woodruff unlimbered his battery and began firing on Lyon's advancing column. During the fighting, young Weaver began walking away from his gun when a solid shot crushed his chest and arm. Woodruff ran to his stricken friend and immediately called for a surgeon, but Weaver died shortly afterward. He was probably the first Arkansan to be killed in the Civil War. The Pulaski battery played a prominent role in stopping Lyon's initial attack, and it remained on the field providing fire support as the Confederates tried unsuccessfully to dislodge the Federals from Bloody Hill. (*Photo courtesy of the Arkansas History Commission*)

Clem McCulloch, shown in uniform on May 18, 1861, with his friend Chaplain William Buford, joined the Van Buren Frontier Guards in 1861. The unit became part of the Third regiment of Arkansas State Troops which fought at Wilson's Creek. McCulloch's captain and two other soldiers died in the fighting. Private John Clark had his arm badly shattered, and Private George Clark was shot through both legs. McCulloch himself received a slight bayonet wound in the back of his leg. It had been administered by his fellow rebel, Private Frank Hinkle, who had gotten excited and tripped over his own feet. (*Photo courtesy of the Washington County Historical Society*)

At sunrise on August 10, the Hempstead Rifles and the six hundred other men of the Third Arkansas Infantry were startled from their sleep by the booming of artillery and the crackling of small armsfire. General Lyon was advancing and the battle had begun. John R. Gratiot, the newly appointed colonel of the regiment, held his men in reserve until the final Confederate assault against Bloody Hill. The fighting lasted barely twenty-five minutes, but Gratiot lost over a hundred men in the attack. The Rifles suffered sixteen casualties. Two of the injured, George Worsham and Lucky Britt, were hit in the face and badly disfigured. Another soldier, A. L. Warner, had his leg shattered. Within three weeks of the fight the Third Arkansas had disbanded. Some of the soldiers, like Clem McCulloch, would eventually join other units, but Gratiot had seen enough fighting. He never again served in the army. (*Photo courtesy of the Old Washington State Park*)

Sergeant Simon McCown posed for this photograph in the uniform of the Davis Blues, a militia company that he helped organize in Nashville, Arkansas. The men mustered into state service as Company F of the Fifth Arkansas Infantry, under the command of Colonel Thomas P. Dockery. McCown fought at Wilson's Creek, and he and his fellow soldiers were lucky, since the regiment suffered only fourteen casualties out of a total strength of 650 men. (*Photo courtesy of the Arkansas History Commission*)

Fighting alongside Dockery's regiment were Lieutenant Lee M. Ramsaur and six hundred other troopers of Colonel T. J. Churchill's First Arkansas Mounted Rifles. During the battle the unit had forty-two killed and one hundred fifty wounded, which was the largest number of casualties of any Southern unit at Wilson's Creek. Among the severely wounded was Lieutenant Ramsaur, who would not rejoin his unit for several months. (*Photo courtesy of Martha Ramseur Gillham*)

On Christmas Day, 1861, Brigadier General
Samuel Ryan Curtis, a West Pointer who had
earlier left the army to pursue a career as an
engineer and who had recently resigned his
seat in Congress, assumed command of the
Army of the Southwest. He was an ener-
getic officer, and in February, 1862, he repeatedly outmaneuvered the Confederate
forces under McCulloch and Price. By the
end of the month, he had pushed into northwest Arkansas as far south as Sugar Creek,
where he ordered his army to halt and dis-
perse to forage for supplies. He was forced
to make this decision because adequate material for his ten thousand troops could not
be hauled over the two hundred miles of
muddy roads that wound back to his logistical base at Rolla, Missouri. Curtis knew
that he was taking a calculated risk by
dividing his army in the presence of the
enemy, but circumstances left him little
choice. However, he alerted his scattered
forces to be ready to concentrate at Sugar
Creek at the first sign of trouble. (*Photo
courtesy of the State Historical Society of
Missouri*)

In January, 1861, Major General Earl Van Dorn arrived at Little Rock to take command of the newly created Trans-Mississippi District No. 2 which had been established primarily to unify the still feuding Price and McCulloch under one commander. He seemed an ideal choice, for even though he had graduated toward the bottom of the class of '42 at West Point, Van Dorn had served with distinction in both the Indian campaigns and the Mexican War. Before he joined the Confederacy, Van Dorn was a major in the celebrated Second United States Cavalry. Among its officers were Albert Sidney Johnston, Robert E. Lee, and George H. Thomas. Learning that Curtis had dispersed his forces, Van Dorn decided to isolate the First and Second divisions near Bentonville. However, the muddy roads made rapid movement impossible, and the Union column slipped away to Sugar Creek before Van Dorn could bring it to battle. Rather than launch a frontal attack against Curtis' united army, Van Dorn decided to attempt a complicated night march to get around Curtis' right flank. (*Photo courtesy of the Chicago Historical Society*)

On the evening of March 6, under cover of darkness, Lieutenant Colonel Robert McCulloch led the First Battalion of Missouri Cavalry up the Bentonville Detour as part of the vanguard that was to place itself astride the Telegraph Road. McCulloch, a proslavery Democrat, had earlier raised a company for the Missouri State Guard and fought at Wilson's Creek. After the battle, many Missourians had left the service, but McCulloch stayed, informing General Sterling Price that he would remain "to drive the hireling from our soil."[8] His raw recruits, armed with only shotguns, were slowed by the felled trees that Curtis' men had cut along the road and could not get into position to attack until well after sunrise on the 7th. During the fighting, McCulloch's men would dismount and fight alongside General William Slack's infantry against units which included the Fourth Iowa Infantry, and the First Iowa Battery. (*Photo Courtesy of the State Historical Society of Missouri*)

Early that morning, Curtis, learning that at least part of Van Dorn's army was at his rear, issued orders for his entire command to turn around and move northward toward Pea Ridge. Major James A. Williamson, the Adjutant of the Fourth Iowa Infantry, was part of the Fourth Division which moved against Van Dorn's left wing on the Telegraph Road. For almost three hours, the regiment stood its ground under terrible fire from rebel infantry and artillery. That evening the regiment marched back to camp, refilled their cartridge boxes, cleaned their guns, and returned to the field. The regiment had suffered 160 casualties, including Major Williamson, who was slightly wounded. (*Photo courtesy of Roger Davis*)

Sergeant William Main was with the Third Iowa Battery which fought at Pea Ridge. On the morning of March 7, the gunners went into action on Curtis' right wing. Within ten minutes, one gun had been disabled, and several men were wounded. With the support of the Ninth Iowa Infantry, the battery held its ground until the Confederate artillery had put nine more guns out of action. An infantry attack, which included McCulloch's battalion, then forced the battery back about three hundred yards where it continued firing until "an immense force of the enemy's infantry" charged the battery and carried off one more gun.[9] During the fighting, the battery's captain, William Hayden, had two horses shot from under him. (*Photo courtesy of Roger Davis*)

On the night of March 6, thirty-three-year-old Private William Holcombe waited for his turn to cross Sugar Creek on the two narrow poles that served as a slippery footbridge for the infantry. Holcombe, the son of a Methodist minister, was farming in Washington County with his wife and children when the war began. On November 1, 1861, he had enlisted as a private in Company G, Fifteenth Arkansas Infantry. His regiment was part of General Ben McCulloch's forces that were ordered to follow behind Sterling Price's Missourians who were inching their way up the Bentonville Detour. Early that morning, the regiment finally crossed the creek, but it was too late for the Arkansas troops to reach the Telegraph Road. At about 8 p.m. the Fifteenth went into battle west of Pea Ridge near Leetown. During the fighting, the regiment was ambushed by Union infantry and forced to retreat, but it soon rallied and held its ground. In the attack, Holcombe was slightly wounded, but he remained with his company when it marched to join the remaining Confederates on the Telegraph Road. (*Photo courtesy of the Washington County Historical Society*)

During the early hours of March 7, 1862, Colonel Stan Watie led his Second Cherokee Mounted Rifles up the road with General James McIntosh's cavalry. Suddenly a Union battery hidden in a cluster of trees opened fire on the moving column. With "shrill whoops and yelling like demons," the Indians and Texas cavalry charged the startled Union artillerymen and captured the battery. The Indians, who had never seen such huge guns, seemed to think that the weapons were "endowed with supernatural powers." Finally they set fire to the carriages and when the guns were lying useless in the ashes, they proudly announced "No more boom.—Good."[10] When a second battery opened fire on the Indians, they fled in confusion toward the woods and remained there until the battle ended. (*Photo courtesy of the UALR Archives*)

Brigadier General James McIntosh, a West Pointer who had graduated last in the class of 1849, enjoyed a successful career in the Confederate army. At the Battle of Wilson's Creek he led the Second Arkansas Mounted Rifles with distinction and General McCulloch praised him as an officer who seemed to be "wherever the balls flew thickest."[11] He quickly became a favorite of McCulloch, who appointed him brigadier general and gave him command of the Confederate cavalry. On March 7, 1862, he fell into line of battle at Leetown. Early in the morning, the fighting was particularly vicious as McCulloch tried to overwhelm the smaller forces of Colonel Peter Osterhaus. That af-

ternoon, McCulloch, who disliked wearing his Confederate uniform and preferred his velvet coat, rode forward to reconnoiter when Peter Pelican of the Thirty-sixth Illinois Infantry spotted the general and fired. McCulloch fell from his saddle mortally wounded and McIntosh assumed command. McIntosh, at the head of his troops, immediately charged the retreating Federal infantry, and within minutes he too was shot and killed. In the confusion, the Confederate advance began to falter and Union reinforcements soon arrived to secure the Federal position. (*Photo courtesy of the UALR Archives*)

Sergeant Charles S. Squires, Company G, Thirty-seventh Illinois Infantry, was part of the Second Brigade, Third Division, that reinforced Osterhaus' men who were in a desperate fight with McCulloch's infantry. About 1 P.M., the brigade began to advance against the Third Louisiana, the Fourteenth and Fifteenth Arkansas, and the Indian Brigade. The line moved slowly until they were about sixty yards from the Confederates. Both sides opened fire simultaneously and continued firing until the sun went down "amid the roar of artillery and the rattle of musketry." The Arkansas regiments were thrown into confusion and fell back on the Louisianians who also became disorganized. That evening, some of the weary Confederates remained on the field and a few men "burrowed among heaps of dry forest-leaves" to help protect them from the chilling mountain air.[12] Meanwhile, other Confederate units were moving up the Bentonville Detour to join Price's soldiers on the Telegraph Road. Across the field the Thirty-seventh Illinois withdrew about two miles and went into camp. The regiment had lost 133 men. (*Photo courtesy of the Western Historical Collection, University of Oklahoma*)

68

Private Calvin Grier Oates was in Company B, Second Arkansas Mounted Rifles, when the regiment deployed for battle at Leetown. There, Confederate and Union units fought a series of isolated and largely uncoordinated engagements. Finally, the sudden deaths of McCulloch and McIntosh threw the Confederates into confusion and they were driven back. The Second Arkansas had six men killed and fourteen wounded. Twenty-three other soldiers, including Private Oates, were captured. That evening the remaining troopers of the Second Arkansas marched to join Price's troops on the Telegraph Road. During the next day's fighting, the Second remained in reserve. (*Photo courtesy of Tami Tidwell*)

By the morning of March 8, Van Dorn had finally succeeded in concentrating most of his infantry on the Telegraph Road, and he was preparing to resume the attack when he learned that the army's reserve munitions train had accidentally been left behind. Without those wagons, Van Dorn could not continue the attack. Now he could only try to halt the impending Union advance and then retreat. The morning's fighting began with an artillery duel, and Private George Coombs and his fellow gunners in the Third Iowa Battery fired furiously at the Confederates. Van Dorn's troops tried to slow the advance, without much success. The Third Iowa Battery, supported by Union infantry, soon drove back to its original position of the previous day and recovered all but three of the lost guns. Van Dorn's defeated army broke off contact and began its long retreat to the Arkansas River. However, after two days of hard fighting the Union army was in no condition to pursue, and most of the exhausted soldiers remained on the battlefield. The gunners of the Third Iowa Battery had fired twelve hundred shells, suffered nineteen casualties, and had twenty-three horses killed. (*Photo courtesy of Roger Davis*)

On November 29, 1862, General James
Blunt, a Kansas physician who had earlier
fought as a Jayhawker in Bleeding Kansas,
marched his seven-thousand-man division
into Cane Hill. During the past few weeks,
his soldiers had routed the ill-equipped and
poorly trained Confederates who had recently tried to invade southern Missouri,
and he had sent them scurrying back across
the Boston Mountains. Because Blunt could
not adequately supply his forces south of
the mountains, he halted the advance, but
he knew that the rebels would be back.
(*Photo courtesy of Special Collections, David
Mullins Library, University of Arkansas,
Fayetteville*)

71

On December 3, 1862, Major General Thomas C. Hindman began moving his ten thousand troops northward toward Cane Hill. The column itself was short of ammunition and the men carried only enough food for seven days at half rations. Several thousand more remained behind because they had no weapons and no shoes. The recent fiasco had already shown that his soldiers' morale was dangerously low, and that their training, leadership, and equipment were inadequate to take the offensive. Such facts were lost on Hindman and he was still determined to winter in Missouri. Because of their desperate condition, the army could only advance about twelve miles per day. On the evening of December 6, Hindman arrived at Cane Hill only to learn that a Union relief column of eight thousand soldiers under General Francis J. Herron was a scant twenty miles away at Fayetteville. Faced with this new threat, Hindman decided that he would leave a small force to pin Blunt, and then move toward Fayetteville to attack Herron's column. If Herron could be defeated, then Hindman would be squarely astride Blunt's line of communications and in an excellent position to destroy him in detail. It was a good plan, and by 4 A.M., Hindman's columns were in motion away from Cane Hill and toward Fayetteville. He had already informed his soldiers that the enemy was "made up of Pin Indians, free Negroes, Southern Tories, Kansas Jayhawkers, and hired Dutch Cut-throats."[13] (*Photo courtesy of the UALR Archives*)

Twenty-five-year-old Brigadier General Francis J. Herron had already seen his share of hard fighting in the Trans-Mississippi West. In 1861, he had mustered in as a captain in the First Iowa Infantry, a unit that later lost 155 men at Wilson's Creek. At Pea Ridge, he was Lieutenant Colonel of the Ninth Iowa Infantry when the regiment suffered 218 casualties. Herron was wounded and captured in the fight. Thirty years later he would receive the Congressional Medal of Honor for his heroism at Pea Ridge. On December 3, 1862, Herron received orders to march immediately to Blunt's assistance. While Hindman's men moved slowly over the Boston Mountains, Herron drove his relief column southward at the rate of almost forty miles per day. On the night of December 6, 1862, his exhausted soldiers reached Fayetteville. The next day he planned to unite with Blunt's forces at Cane Hill. (*Photo courtesy of Greg McMahon*)

73

Lieutenant Charles W. DeWolf was with the Seventh Missouri Cavalry when it began its advance toward Cane Hill. Coming up the road were eighteen hundred Confederate cavalrymen, the vanguard of Hindman's army which was now attempting to isolate and defeat Herron. DeWolf had just sat down for a breakfast of oysters and sardines when a trooper dashed up shouting that the regiment was "surrounded and all cut to pieces."[14] DeWolf's heart sank, and soon, other frightened soldiers without saddles and firearms were streaming to the rear. Federal infantry finally stopped the rout, but the Seventh Missouri had lost 142 prisoners. Later that day about one hundred other stragglers made it to Prairie Grove, but they were not in condition to fight. (*Photo courtesy of the Arkansas Historical Association*)

When the war began, Edward Gee Miller, a student at the University of Wisconsin, enlisted for three months' service. He mustered out on August 21, 1861, and returned to his studies. In May, 1862, the United States again asked for more troops, and Miller mustered in as Captain of Company G, Twentieth Wisconsin Infantry. He had marched with Herron's column, and on December 7, 1862, the exhausted soldiers fell into line opposite the Confederate infantry at Prairie Grove. That day the Twentieth Wisconsin listed 50 dead, 153 wounded, and 13 missing, the highest casualty figures of any Union outfit in the battle. On December 9, Miller served as Officer of the Day and supervised the burying of the Wisconsin dead. "The men of our regiment," he wrote in his diary, "were buried in a 'soldier's grave,' each with a headboard with his name, company, and regiment cut plainly on it."[15] (*Photo courtesy of the Washington County Historical Society*)

Colonel William H. Cloud, commander of the Third Brigade, First Division, Army of the Frontier, was lying in line of battle near Cane Hill on the morning of December 7. General Hindman had left Colonel J. C. Monroe's cavalry brigade behind to mask his movement toward Herron. He had ordered the colonel to pin Blunt down and "press him vigorously" if it appeared that the Union column was about to withdraw toward Herron. However, Monroe, by his own admission, "moved slowly and cautiously."[16] His timidity freed Blunt to march to the sound of the artillery fire at Prairie Grove to reinforce Herron, who was being pressed hard by the Confederate infantry. Cloud's brigade reached Prairie Grove about 2 P.M. and immediately went into action. The Third Brigade arrived in time to protect the Twentieth Iowa, which had been routed by the Confederate infantry, but they too were forced to retreat several hundred yards before stabilizing their line behind a long fence. Repeated Confederate infantry attacks failed to dislodge Cloud's men, and when darkness fell, the fighting died down. (*Photo courtesy of the J. N. Heiskell Historical Collection, UALR Archives*)

Captain Tom Thomson was a member of the Thirty-third Arkansas Infantry that fought at Prairie Grove. He had first enlisted as a private in the Fifteenth Arkansas Infantry, but Thomson was on leave when his regiment surrendered on February 15, 1862, at Fort Donelson, Tennessee. In the summer of 1862, he joined the newly raised Thirty-third Arkansas. Like many of the units at Prairie Grove, Thomson's outfit had no uniforms and most of the men were armed with only shotguns. Even these weapons were in short supply and Thomson's company had only enough shotguns to arm half his company. About 11 A.M., Hindman ordered his weary infantry, which had already marched fifteen miles, to form a defensive line at Prairie Grove. The Thirty-third arrived on the field that morning, but it didn't see much action until about 2 P.M., when Blunt's troops began arriving. Thomson wrote that suddenly the Pin Indians charged and "set up one of the most horrible yells I ever heard."[17] The Thirty-third repulsed the attack, suffering only two killed, eleven wounded, and twelve missing. Hindman's infantry managed to hold the field until dark, at which time he withdrew southward. (*Photo courtesy of the Public Library of Camden and Ouachita County, Arkansas*)

While Tom Thomson withdrew with the retreating rebels, Major William G. Thompson of the Twentieth Iowa Infantry, rested on the field at Prairie Grove. During the battle he had watched with pride as his regiment advanced with a cheer against the Confederate infantry. Just at sundown "one of the cowardly curs . . . took good aim" and shot Thompson in the hip. The ball chipped the bone and damaged the "leaders" before it came out in his groin. The next day he rode in a wagon to Fayetteville and found himself in the parlor of the "finest house" in town.[18] This photo was taken when he mustered into the service at Marion, Iowa, in the fall of 1861. (*Photo courtesy of the Washington County Historical Society*)

William Wallace Crump mustered into the army on February 15, 1862, as a Second Lieutenant in Company D, Twenty-seventh Arkansas Infantry, which had not been completely armed prior to Prairie Grove, and when it started northward, most of the men still carried an old hunting rifle or a shotgun. On the march, Colonel J. R. Shaler went to General Hindman and informed him that "it would be counted no less than murder" to send the regiment into battle without the "arms to defend themselves." He begged the commander to send the Twenty-seventh back to Van Buren, and Hindman agreed. After the battle the regiment watched as several hundred Federal prisoners were being marched to Fort Smith. After looking them over, one rebel soldier declared that "the fellows look like they have been having plenty to eat before they were captured. But if they stay with us long, and are fed on the same kind and quantity of rations we get their faces will begin to look slim and lean like ours." The Twenty-seventh marched to Little Rock with what remained of Hindman's army. Suffering "untold misery, hunger, and cold," the remains of the Twenty-seventh Infantry staggered into the capital on January 14, 1863.[19] (*Photo courtesy of Mrs. Lucille Long Rogers*)

Chapter 3

Helena and the War along the Mississippi

After the Union victory at Pea Ridge in March, 1862, only General Curtis' decision to regroup his forces in Missouri prevented Arkansas from falling easy prey to Federal forces in the spring and summer of 1862. Albert Pike withdrew the men under his command to the Indian Territory, while the main force of the Confederate army retreated to the Arkansas River and Little Rock, and then moved on to the Mississippi. As Confederate General Earl Van Dorn withdrew from Little Rock, he took with him everything that could be of use to the enemy. Confederate leadership seemed to have abandoned the state.

Curtis did not begin an immediate move into Arkansas because the northwestern route had proven a dead end. He now looked for an alternative route that would make possible the provisioning of his men. The need to support his twenty thousand men over a long overland supply line dictated the strategy he chose. Instead of following in Van Dorn's path, Curtis moved his army to White River, occupying Batesville on

May 4. The White River offered him an alternate supply line if Union gunboats and supply boats could be brought up river to him. By May 31, Curtis had pushed to within thirty-five miles of Little Rock.

Only heroic measures could have stopped Curtis. The Confederate hero of the hour turned out to be Brigadier General Thomas C. Hindman from Helena, ordered to assume command of the state on May 31. Hindman, then east of the Mississippi, moved to Memphis where he procured arms and supplies, as well as one million dollars from local banks. Moving by steamboat, Hindman confiscated everything that he could use to fight with and brought it with him to Little Rock. Hindman proved to be as ruthless a military commander as he had been a politician. Almost immediately, he issued orders allowing individuals to form groups known as partisan rangers to cut off "federal pickets, scouts, foraging parties, and trains."[1] He also raised additional troops by enforcing the Conscription Act, which, accord-

79

ing to John Brown of Camden, "was forcing thousands of unwilling men from their homes."[2] He then declared martial law and ordered his commanders to purchase or impress any supplies that they needed. He also issued orders to destroy all cotton that might be in danger of falling into enemy hands and to treat anyone who resisted as a traitor. When some of his impressed troops tried to desert, he tried four of them as traitors and "ordered them shot to death in front of the troops and saw the order executed."[3] Such excesses may have been necessary if Arkansas was to survive Curtis' invasion, but Hindman's actions were met by a howl of protest among Arkansans who began pressuring officials at Richmond to remove the commander.

Curtis was in an awkward position. The rear of his army was under constant attack by partisans who disrupted his line of supply. Hindman encouraged this activity with his Order Number 17 that gave military authority to guerilla units. The Federal officer's hope for relief from the river was dashed on June 17 when Confederate forces at St. Charles successfully stalled efforts at opening up the White when they took the gunboat *Mound City* out of action with a lucky shot through her boilers. With a Confederate army under General Albert Rust moving on his rear, Curtis marched his army successfully overland to Helena on the river where he could be supported.

With the Union army in Helena, the war in the central part of the state would bog down into a stalemate for over a year. Neither Hindman nor Curtis would be involved in it, however. On July 16, 1862, Major General Theophilus Holmes replaced Hindman as the commander of the Trans-Mississippi Department. Hindman then assumed command of the District of Arkansas which was under the control of Holmes. On September 19, 1862, Curtis received orders to report to St. Louis to assume command of the Department of Missouri. Neither Holmes nor the successive

Union commanders in Helena appeared anxious to fight.

The lack of action worked to the advantage of the Union forces. As a major supply point for operations along the Mississippi, Helena was fortified heavily and filled with troops. One Union soldier noted that the town of Helena practically disappeared as his fellow soldiers took everything possible to construct habitable dwellings for their long stay. The base at Helena became a staging area for Union activities that aimed at opening the Mississippi to New Orleans. In addition, Federal forces staged profitable raids against Confederate plantations along the rivers of Arkansas, seizing cotton and slaves. Confederate General Holmes realized that the occupation of the town could be an immense advantage to the Union. The Federals threatened an invasion of Arkansas, thus tying up troops that were needed in other theaters; they controlled trade and consequently sentiment in a large area of Arkansas; and they possessed an important depot for troops being used by General Grant in his operations against Vicksburg.

The importance of Helena was apparent when naval and land forces operating out of that town captured Arkansas Post, the last major Confederate position in Arkansas along the Mississippi, on January 11, 1863. Considering the forces that the Federals could bring into a fight there, most Confederates on the ground considered the position doomed. When General Holmes ordered General Thomas J. Churchill to "hold the place until every man is dead," the soldiers in the fortification were not convinced it was worth the fight.[4] William W. Heartsill wrote of the order, "if 'Granny' Holmes was down here where he could smell a little gunpowder he would get better of the 'hold on' fit which has so recently seized him AT LITTLE ROCK."[5] Heartsill was a better judge of the situation than Holmes, for the Confederates did not hold on. When the fortification fell, the Union forces had access to the interior of the state. The Federals could move their infantry up the rivers supported by gunboats. Only Union concern with operations in the Vicksburg area postponed this offensive.

While threatening an invasion, Union forces staged repeated raids into the interior. Intended to disrupt the Confederate economy, these raids led to the development of an extensive operation in blackmarket cotton along the Mississippi. The town of Helena became a major center of this trade. Federal officers traded contraband cotton with anyone who would make a deal, including blacks, white Unionists, and Confederate sympathizers. The cotton business quickly undermined the morale of soldiers stationed in the town. Officers sent their men into the interior on raids that produced profits for the officers and death for many of the enlisted men. Henry Ankeny of the Fourth Iowa Infantry wrote of the trade, "Had we used half the force and industry to put the rebels down in Arkansas [that] we have [used] to steal cotton it would have been better for the nation and the Army."[6]

The cotton raiders brought thousands of slaves into Union lines along with the sought-after cotton. These joined at least two thousand black refugees who had come to Helena in 1862 after having joined Curtis' march down the White River. The Union army took these people as another way of upsetting the local economy. Blacks came with the army seeking freedom. Freedom in Helena, however, was accompanied by great privation. There they were treated badly by the Union soldiers, and left to survive as best they could. Helena remained a refuge throughout the war, but many who sought freedom there found only death caused by disease and a lack of adequate food.

Surrounded by their enemy, with thousands of men poured into a small segment of land only about ten miles long and perhaps two miles wide, the town felt the strain as conditions deteriorated. Some of the soldiers from the Thirty-

third Iowa Infantry called it "Hell-in-Arkansas." In the winter, the soldiers and the refugees were beset by constant rain and the mud that came with it. One observer noted that when it rained, the streets of Helena were almost impassable for persons on foot. Worse for most soldiers, the perpetual damp provided a breeding place for diseases that constantly plagued the occupying army.

The military inaction by Confederate authorities finally ended in the summer of 1863 when Holmes moved his army from Little Rock to the edges of Helena. He hoped to provide relief to the Confederate garrison besieged at Vicksburg or at least keep the Mississippi closed by wresting Helena from Federal control. He finally attacked on July 4, the day before Vicksburg surrendered, thus sacrificing his army without providing relief for that place and failing to gain control of Helena to blockade the Mississippi. Others questioned whether his goal of closing the Mississippi would work. The *Patriot* attacked Holmes' plan as a blunder, "if given to us to-day, we could not hold it an hour."[7]

The Confederate assault on Helena proved a costly disaster. While Confederate forces successfully reached Federal lines, they were repeatedly thrown back. Holmes' attacking army of 7,646 men reported 173 killed, 687 wounded, and 776 missing. The 239 killed, wounded and missing in Prentiss' army of 4,129 men meant the defenders had been barely bloodied. Holmes had no alternative but to take his badly beaten army back to Little Rock. F. R. Earle of the Thirty-fourth Arkansas Infantry wrote home from Searcy about the business, "The most important item of all is that we were repulsed and retreated, and kept on retreating until now."[8] All along the way his unit was depleted by desertions as many Confederate Arkansans finally concluded that their presence in the army was no longer needed.

The Union victory at Helena left the Federal

forces firmly in control of the river approaches to Arkansas. The invasion feared by Holmes would come in due time. In August, 1863, a Union army under General Frederick Steele moved up the Arkansas River, finally ready for the attack upon Little Rock that had been stalled in the spring of 1862. At the same time, another force in the northwestern part of the state began to move toward Van Buren and Fort Smith to establish permanent control of that gateway to the Indian Territory. With Steele's campaign against the capital of the state, the war in Arkansas would enter a new stage.

General Theophilus Hunter Holmes had the misfortune of commanding Arkansas during the disasters that took place in 1863. Holmes had been named commander of the Trans-Mississippi Department on October 10, 1862, and although reluctant to take the position, was finally persuaded to do so. Throughout his service in Arkansas, the general was ill, and he appeared ill-suited to the demands of his office. His orders show him to be prone to bombast and inattentive to details. After ordering Churchill's command at Arkansas Post to "hold out till help arrived or until all dead,"[9] he expressed relief that his "hasty order was rendered negatory before the brave Churchill was reduced to the *ultima ratio*—cutting his way through such immense odds. It never occurred to me when the order was issued that such an overpowering command would be devoted to an end so trivial."[10] After marching an army to the environs of Helena in July, 1863, he noted that "information disclosed that the place was very much more difficult of access, and the fortifications very much stronger, than I had supposed before undertaking the expedition."[11] He attacked anyway. When Steele marched on Little Rock, Holmes would be indisposed. He was finally removed from his command in 1864 and was sent to North Carolina where he remained for the rest of the war. (*Photo courtesy of the Library of Congress*)

As Hindman's disintegrating army struggled toward Little Rock, another disaster unfolded at the Arkansas Post on the Arkansas River. There, General Theophilus Holmes had hastily constructed Ft. Hindman to block any attempted riverine advance by the Union army. Throughout the fall of 1862 he had scraped together troops such as Captain Sam J. Richardson's Independent Company of Texas Cavalry to garrison the fort. Richardson and his men had been at the post less than six weeks when, on January 11, 1863, the fort fell to a combined attack of fifteen gunboats and thirty thousand Union soldiers. Even though the assault was a side show to the Vicksburg Campaign, the Confederates had lost Richardson and five thousand prisoners that they desperately needed to defend Arkansas. (*Photo courtesy of the UALR Archives*)

Helena, on the Mississippi River, became the destination of General Curtis' Army of the Southwest in the early summer of 1862. Unable to pursue his campaign against Little Rock after efforts to resupply the army along the White River failed, Curtis chose to move to the Mississippi and establish a base. The small town of frame houses had recently suffered from an overflow of the river, and the Federal troops were not impressed with their new home. One would write, "It is a low muddy place with numerous ponds of filthy green looking water."[12] Water and mud would plague the soldiers occupying Helena through the rest of the war. This photograph was taken later in the war, but it shows Helena as it must have appeared to the soldiers of Curtis' army as they marched across Crowley's Ridge into the town. This picture, made during the flood of 1864, was made from the ridge looking towards the southeast, showing the Mississippi River in the distance and the major portion of the town. The road running between homes to the right of the picture ran to the west and became the Upper Little Rock Road. (*Photo courtesy of the Phillips County Museum, Helena, Arkansas*)

Nearly twenty thousand Federal troops crowded into Helena in the summer of 1862. The town fell prey to their efforts at creating comfortable quarters in their new surroundings. They occupied abandoned homes and businesses. Outbuildings were taken apart as the soldiers appropriated lumber to improve their camps. The infantry units camped along the bluffs to the west of the town, guarding the principal roads. When it became obvious that Curtis did not intend to move, they expanded their tents in all manners imaginable. The squad shown mustering in this photograph had constructed a shed along the front of their tents, possibly for use as a dining or a living area. Captain Thomas N. Stevens of the Twenty-eighth Wisconsin Infantry described the interior of one such tent. He wrote to his children, "It is as big as a bedroom, and I have a stove in it, and a little table, made by driving four sticks into the ground, and putting a box on the top—bottom side up. Then I have a box to sit on when I eat, and write letters. I spread my blankets on the ground inside the tent and sleep on them."[13] Stevens had "carpeted" his tent with shakes and built up the sides with lumber from the town. (*Photo courtesy of the Arkansas History Commission*)

After its occupation, Helena became a major Federal base along the Mississippi. It was garrisoned through the rest of the war and was a base for all operations into Arkansas. The soldiers turned the little river town into a city of small huts to permanently house the occupying forces. The huts shown above were built on a ridge west of the town and behind the Helena home of Confederate general Gideon Pillow. Most of the huts were of log construction with fireplaces. They were large enough to house a squad or a mess. Minos Miller of the Thirty-third Iowa Infantry occupied a building designed for two persons in the summer of 1863. He described it as comfortable, although with only a few amenities. The eight-foot-square building contained a bunk, four stools, and a writing desk. (*Photo courtesy of the Arkansas History Commission*)

Occupied Helena always housed a cavalry brigade, usually elements of two or more cavalry regiments. The only place suited for the cavalry was along a flat piece of land to the north of the town and outside of the protective levee. From July, 1862, until June, 1863, the Third Iowa Cavalry was one of the units assigned to Helena. Like the infantry units, the Third Iowa built a camp consisting of regulation tents and makeshift log cabins and sheds. This photograph is of the unit's camp and shows the variety of construction employed. (*Photo courtesy of the State Historical Society of Iowa, Special Collections*)

For the army occupying Helena there was little to do during the winter, 1862–1863. Operations in Arkansas were restricted to raids against encircling Confederate units while the main thrust of Federal action was towards Vicksburg, farther south on the Mississippi. To weaken the Confederate war effort and also to obtain much needed cotton, Union forces staged numerous raids upon plantations along the Mississippi, White, and Arkansas rivers. On these raids they seized both cotton and slaves which were brought to Helena. Officers of the Federal units engaged in an extensive cotton trade during this period. Some of the trade was legal, much of it illegal. H. P. Coolidge was a Unionist who continued to operate his store in Helena after Curtis occupied the town. During the war he engaged in the buying and selling of cotton. This picture shows his store at some time during the military occupation, showing cotton arriving and on the store porch. (*Photo courtesy of the Arkansas History Commission*)

The *Eastport* was one of the naval vessels engaged in supporting Union efforts to seize Confederate cotton. During her career the gunboat helped to capture over fourteen thousand cotton bales. Ironically, the *Eastport* was built as a Confederate vessel, but seized on February 7, 1862, while yet uncompleted. The *Eastport* was taken from Cerro Gordo on the Tennessee River to Cairo, Illinois, where workmen sheathed her in iron and outfitted her with four 32-pound guns and an equal number of Dahlgren rifles. She was stationed at Helena from June, 1863, until the next spring. This photograph shows her off of the wharf at Helena sometime in the spring of 1864. In March, 1864, the *Eastport* left the area and joined the Red River expedition. On April 15, while operating on the Red River, she was struck by a torpedo and destroyed by her crew to prevent falling into Confederate hands. (*Photo courtesy of the Arkansas History Commission*)

The cotton trade at Helena became a scandal among the troops stationed there. Many enlisted men thought that their officers were more concerned with buying and selling cotton than fighting the war. John Phelps, sent to Helena to act as governor of Arkansas, noted one officer allegedly traded contrabands back to Confederates in return for cotton. In September, 1862, the Treasury Department issued orders that attempted to impose regulations on the cotton trade. Movement of cotton was still possible, but only under Treasury Department control. As a result, the Treasury opened a customs house at Helena to oversee the continued trade that took place between the lines of the armies. (*Photo courtesy of the Arkansas History Commission*)

Along with cotton, Federal raiders brought thousands of contraband slaves back to Helena. While the seizure of these slaves deprived the Confederacy of their service, the Federal occupying forces were ill-equipped to provide for them or to use them. The able-bodied men were put to work cutting wood for boats on the rivers. In the spring of 1863 they were also enlisted in the Federal army. For women, children, and the elderly, there was not much to do. Many starved, many died from disease. In the town one way of surviving was to labor—as cooks, washerwomen, or seamstresses. This photograph shows a group of contrabands gathered behind the United States Customs House. Each day prospective employers would hire workers from among this force. (*Photo courtesy of the Phillips County Museum, Helena, Arkansas*)

After the capture of Helena, the town became the center of efforts by President Abraham Lincoln to restore Arkansas to the Union. In July, 1862, Lincoln appointed John S. Phelps of Missouri as military governor of the state. Because Union forces did not move against Little Rock, Phelps had nothing to do. Phelps went to Helena in August, 1862, but soon returned to Missouri. Nothing more was done to restore loyal government in Arkansas until after the capture of Little Rock in September, 1863. On December 8, 1863, Lincoln issued his amnesty proclamation for Arkansas. Thus encouraged, local Unionists moved to hold a constitutional convention the following January. Unionists at Helena were prominent in these efforts. The Episcopal church at Helena was one of the sites of their meetings. On January 2, 1864, the building was used for a meeting that elected delegates to a state constitutional convention to write a constitution acceptable to Congress. (*Photo courtesy of the Phillips County Musuem, Helena, Arkansas*)

Unionists in Arkansas also used Helena as a point for pursuing their efforts to organize loyal military units. One of these units was the Second Arkansas Cavalry. Many Arkansans had come to Helena with Curtis' army in the spring of 1862. John E. Phelps, son of the state's military governor, was assigned to create this unit. Enough men to constitute a regiment with full strength were not obtained, however, until the spring of 1864. At that time Phelps' organization was recognized as the Second Arkansas, and Phelps was named colonel of the regiment. Shown with his wife, this picture of Phelps was apparently made at Helena sometime in 1863. (*Photo courtesy of the Arkansas History Commission*)

In the fall and spring of 1862–1863, small units of Confederate cavalry and guerilla groups harassed the Federal forces occupying Helena. Always fearful that the activity of these groups would mask a major drive against the town, Federal commanders ordered infantry and cavalry to scout the surrounding countryside. No major battles were fought, but such operations typified the war in Arkansas and were often bloody affairs. Elements of the Third Iowa Cavalry, shown in formation on the cavalry parade grounds at Helena, were involved in a typical engagement of this sort on May 1, 1863. Ten miles away from the lines at Helena on a scout, the unit was surrounded by guerillas and forced to fight its way back to the protection of the town's forts. The small affair cost the unit forty men killed and wounded. Captain Thomas N. Stevens witnessed the hurried return. He wrote, "Riderless horses, too, came in with them, some wounded themselves, their saddles and sides red with the blood of the 'brave boys' who had gone out with them in the morning, but who were now either dead or disabled. . . . They were badly cut up, and badly scared I should judge from what I can learn thus far."[14] (*Photos courtesy of the State Historical Society of Iowa, Special Collections*)

The long-feared Confederate attack on Helena finally came in July, 1863. Lieutenant General Theophilus H. Holmes wanted to destroy the garrison there to help the beleaguered Confederate garrison at Vicksburg, to keep the Mississippi River closed should Vicksburg fall, and to remove the persistent threat to Arkansas. Holmes planned his attack for July 4. The plan was simple, to throw the weight of his army, estimated by the Federals at between fifteen and twenty thousand men, against the garrison's fortifications astride the two main roads to Little Rock. Two brigades under Major General Sterling Price were to attack Graveyard Hill, protected by Federal Battery C, and one brigade led by James G. Fagan was to attack Hindman Hill, occupied by another Federal fort, Battery D. At daylight on the fourth, the attack began, but it was not concerted as planned. Fagan's brigade attacked alone against the formidable defenses of Battery D. Placed on a hill behind the home of Confederate General Thomas Hindman, a clear field of fire had been prepared to the west. The approach to the battery was obstructed by both a steep slope and trees cut to improve sight and impede an attack. (*Photo courtesy of the Arkansas History Commission*)

Captain Denis Behen, Jr., was regimental quartermaster for the Thirty-seventh Arkansas Infantry and was present at Helena on July 4. The Thirty-seventh, Hawthorne's regiment, Brooks's Thirty-fourth, and King's Thirty-fifth formed Fagan's brigade that opened the attack and encountered the formidable works of Battery D. While the brigade took several lines of rifle pits, the attack was blunted by both the fire encountered and problems with the terrain. Major T. H. Blacknall described the assault of the Thirty-seventh, writing, "The ground at this point was almost impassable—an old road and deep ravine full of timber, which scattered our men—and it was impossible to keep in line; but we succeeded in getting through after remaining in the timber and hollows nearly two hours, under a heavy fire, and made a charge, when, the enemy giving way, we entered the rifle-pits. Here many of our men fell, perfectly exhausted from overheat."[15] Receiving no support, Fagan was unable to continue and finally fell back. Of the 432 members of the Thirty-seventh, 217 were lost in the action. Behen, seated on the left, is shown with his friends, Captain Foote (standing) and Captain Robards. (*Photo courtesy of the Arkansas History Commission*)

The fighting at Battery C determined the outcome of the Battle of Helena. General Price's two brigades did not make their assault until over an hour after the time ordered by Holmes. Coming up on the position shown here from the other side of the hill, the brigades of Dandridge McRae and M. Monroe Parsons survived withering frontal and flank fire and seized the Federal position. They found that the Federals had disabled the guns at that position and had to have cannon moved up from the rear. While waiting, the Confederates were subjected to continuous fire from Federal siege artillery at Fort Curtis and from the gunboat *Tyler* in the river. At about nine o'clock, Holmes ordered a part of the force occupying Graveyard Hill to support another attack by Fagan on Battery D. Fagan's attack failed, the relief force was stopped, and a Federal counterattack on Graveyard Hill finally pushed the Confederates out of this position before being able to bring up guns that could be used against the Federal fortifications. Gained at great cost, Graveyard Hill and Battery C were given up by the Confederates only six hours after the battle had begun. A general Confederate retreat began shortly afterward. (*Photos courtesy of the Arkansas History Commission*)

Federal superiority in artillery played a major factor in their victory at Helena. Naval guns, siege guns in the fortifications, and field artillery harassed the Confederate attackers and cut them up so badly that they were unable to consolidate their victory at Battery C. The gunboat *Tyler* was the only naval vessel involved in the battle, but the Confederate assaults took place just within the range of her seven guns. Four hundred and thirty-three rounds of 8-inch shells came down on the attacking Confederates. Graveyard Hill received much of the *Tyler's* attention. Although naval gunfire did not prevent the capture of the hill, it littered the ground in front, accounting for perhaps six hundred Confederate casualties. The day after the battle, Minos Miller, a Union officer, visited the field and wrote to his mother that, "the Rebbels was laying thick. Some of them tore all to pieces with shell and some shot through with solid shot. They laid there 24 hours when I seen them last and began to smell bad and look tuff."[16] (*Photo courtesy of the U.S. Naval Historical Center*)

Fort Curtis, an earthwork position reinforced with sandbags, was the key to the Union position at Helena. The fort contained nine 32-pound siege guns mounted on platforms that allowed the guns to fire anywhere on the field. Manned by members of the Thirty-third Missouri Infantry, the guns of Fort Curtis were used against Confederate troops assaulting Batteries C and D. Lieutenant Colonel William H. Heath of the Thirty-third concluded that, "Considering that the gunners in Fort Curtis had had no target practice, the firing from the fort, as well as the batteries, was, in the main, remarkably good."[17] (*Photos courtesy of the Arkansas History Commission*)

Federal field artillery was also effective. Lieutenant Orlo H. Lyon commanded a section of the Third Iowa Battery. Assigned to support Battery D, Lyon turned his 6-pounder on Confederate attackers moving from Battery C against D. His commander concluded that the effectiveness of the unit's fire helped repulse the enemy. Going into the ravine on the afternoon after the attack, Captain Thomas N. Stevens of the Twenty-eighth Wisconsin saw only carnage. He wrote, "It was a sickening sight. The ridges and ravines were thickly strewn with ghastly corpses covered with gore—hands, arms, legs shot away—mutilated in almost every manner by shot and shell—while the moans of the severely wounded could be heard on every side."[18] (*Photo courtesy of the Iowa Historical Society*)

Following the Confederate attack on Helena and the Union victory, serious threats against the Federal position there never occurred again. The town would always be subjected to guerilla actions, but the Confederate army never had a big enough force in the region to mount a full scale assault again. Helena remained a garrison that supported actions in Mississippi and the supply lines into the interior of Arkansas. For the soldiers stationed there, life would remain much as it had when they arrived in 1862. Annual floods and the summer's heat worked to make the town what one Federal called "Hell-in-Arkansas." Broken levees and flooded streets shown in the overflow of March 25, 1864, provided the memory of Helena of many Northern soldiers. (*Photo of broken levee courtesy of Bill Rasp. Others courtesy of the Arkansas History Commission*)

Chapter 4

The Naval War

When the Civil War began, most Northern strategists knew that the South could not be defeated unless the Union could seize control of the Mississippi River and its vast network of tributaries whose meandering waterways penetrated into the heartland of the Western Confederacy. These water routes could provide the avenues along which supplies and Union troops could be moved to reconquer the South, but they could not be utilized until the Union had enough suitable military vessels to drive the Confederates from the rivers. In 1861 the Union had a small blue-water navy, but few of their ships were suitable for service in inland waters. Naval vessels operating at sea needed both speed and long cruising ranges to patrol vast distances. They also had to be seaworthy enough to survive rigorous weather conditions. The United States Navy had been designed to meet those conditions, but these large, deep-draft vessels would be utterly useless on most of the shallow, twisting streams in the west.

There, the ideal craft were the flat bottomed paddle-wheeled river steamers that had been used for decades. These were easily available to Union purchasing agents, and with some work they could be quickly modified for military use. Between 1861 and 1865, the Federals purchased at least eighty such steamers and converted them into gunboats. The Union had an additional twenty-five vessels constructed specifically as gunboats, and used ten others that had been captured from the Confederacy. The flotilla contained every imaginable type of vessel. The most common that were converted to military use were flat bottomed, usually with four-foot drafts and displacements of 150 to 250 tons, driven by stern or side wheels. They were sheathed with thin layers of iron and armed with either Dahlgren or Parrot rifles which commonly fired thirty-two or forty-two pound shells. Yet it was not unusual to see vessels equipped with 12-pound field pieces, 8-inch guns, and howitzers. Occasionally, a boat would be outfitted with weapons like the massive 100-pound Parrot Rifles. There was little attempt to standardize the caliber or type of arms carried, and almost all the boats had a variety. Vessels that were constructed as gunboats were generally larger than the converted steamers and averaged almost 600 tons. These were usually covered with thicker iron, propelled by protected paddle wheels, and had fixed locations for their guns. However, a few with screw propellers and revolving gun turrets were constructed for riverine service.

The largest boat to operate on the western rivers was the 1033-ton *Benton*, a converted snag boat armed with seven 32-pounders and seven 42-pounders. The smallest boat in the flotilla, the captured Confederate steamer *General Sterling Price*, displayed only 38 tons and carried two 12-pound howitzers. Before the war ended, approximately 116 vessels would serve in the flotilla, and 21 would be lost either by accident or by hostile attacks. Two vessels, the *Queen City* and the *Linden*, would be sunk on Arkansas rivers.

The Confederates attempted to counter the Union navy in a variety of ways. The most common tactic was to fortify strategic points along the rivers by using heavy weapons that could match the firepower of the Union gunboats. These points could usually be captured with combined attacks by the Union army and navy, but such operations often endangered the ships. The navy, for example, lost the *Cincinnati* and *Lancaster* to the Vicksburg batteries, and in the spring of 1864, Confederate artillery fire helped destroy the *Signal* and the *Covington* on the Red River. Underwater mines were equally dangerous to

the wooden hulled vessels. Since these devices could be located almost anywhere and were difficult to detect, they were constant sources of concern for the gunboat commanders. The *Cairo* and the *Baron DeKalb*, two of the excellent ironclads constructed by James B. Eads, were sunk by torpedoes on the Yazoo River. The Confederates also tried to challenge the Union riverine forces by outfitting their own gunboats. At least thirty-seven vessels eventually served with the Confederacy on the western waters, but they were no match for the Union navy. Most were destroyed by the Confederates themselves to keep them from falling into Union hands. Only two rebel gunboats ever operated in Arkansas, and both were destroyed by Southerners; these were the *Maurepas*, sunk at St. Charles on June 16, 1862, to block the channel of the White River, and the *Pontchartrain*, which operated on the Arkansas River until shortly after the fall of Little Rock. On October 9, 1863, the Confederates burned the boat to prevent her capture by the Union army.

Shore batteries, torpedoes, and Confederate gunboats did some damage to the western flotilla, but the biggest threat came from the inherent dangers associated with operating wooden hulled vessels on the treacherous waterways. Hidden sandbars, snags, fires, explosions, and collisions were the constant enemies of the gunboats. The Confederates, the rivers, and the boats themselves were all constant dangers with which the Union navy had to contend, but this did not prevent them from controlling the rivers. This control allowed the Northern army to project its power into the heartland of Arkansas.

In the summer of 1861, the Union purchased *Conestoga, Tyler,* and *Lexington,* the first vessels to be outfitted for military service on the western waters. These boats were shallow draft sidewheelers with high-pressure steam engines, and even though the steamers were old, they could be made into serviceable gunboats. Five-inch oak bulkheads were added to protect the crew from small arms fire, but these timbers could provide little defense against artillery shells. The 575-ton *Conestoga* was outfitted with nine heavy guns, and by August, 1861, she and her sister ships were prowling the rivers. *Conestoga* first operated in Arkansas in June, 1862, when she helped capture the Confederate batteries on the White River at St. Charles. She continued to remain on station near the mouths of the Arkansas and White rivers until mid-1863. During the summer, the sweltering temperatures on the rivers made the vessels almost unbearable. The cool weather in the fall gave most of the crew some respite, but those who worked in the engine room still suffered. In November, 1862, one of *Conestoga*'s firemen, Lorenzo Ellsworth, became "overheated by labor and heat from the furnace," suffered a stroke, and had to be discharged from the service.[1] *Conestoga* continued to operate on the Mississippi River and her tributaries until March 5, 1864, when she collided with *General Sterling Price* and sank immediately. (*Photo courtesy of the U.S. Naval Historical Center*)

Forest Rose

Cricket

The *Cricket* and *Forest Rose* are typical examples of a number of small vessels that the Union navy purchased to operate on the western waters. These lightly armed, shallow draft vessels were commonly known as tinclads because of the thin layers of iron that were added to protect their frail timbers. Throughout the war such vessels convoyed transports, captured small steamers, and patrolled the rivers to impede the movement of Confederate soldiers and supplies. *Forest Rose's* experiences near Helena between February 14 and 18, 1863, are good examples of the duties of these small vessels. On February 14, she seized the stern wheeler *Chippewa Valley* with 118 bales of cotton. Four days later, while steaming past Buck Island, guerillas fired at the *Forest Rose.* She landed a small party and destroyed a dwelling, store house, and the slave quarters. The landing party also seized 21 blacks, 4 animals, 500 pounds of bacon, 154 blankets, and captured 5 prisoners. Vessels such as these were especially useful for patrol duties on smaller tributaries where larger armored gunboats with deeper drafts could not travel. The *Cricket,* with her four-foot draft and six 24-pound howitzers, was perfect for such operations. On August 13, 1863, the *Cricket,* accompanied by the *Marmora, Lexington* and two hundred infantry, left Clarendon on such an expedition. The flotilla planned to push up the White River to Jacksonport to learn the location of General Sterling Price's army, to destroy the telegraph at Des Arc, and to capture two steamboats, *Kaskashia* and *Tom Sugg.* At Des Arc, Union forces burned a large warehouse filled with cornmeal and destroyed the telegraph line for nearly half a mile. The next morning, the commanding officer, Lieutenant George M. Bache, dispatched the *Cricket* with 150 soldiers up the "narrow and torturous" Little Red River in search of the two steamboats.[2] Meanwhile the *Lexington* and *Marmora* steamed to Augusta and confirmed the location of Price's troops. The *Cricket* continued steaming up the Little Red until she surprised and captured the two steamboats at Searcy Landing. She also destroyed General John S. Marmaduke's pontoon bridge. On the return trip, rebel troops attacked the steamer near West Point and wounded nine persons. Soon the two captured steamboats were being used to transport Union supplies and troops while the Confederates had lost two boats on the White River. Small actions like these occurred almost daily on the western waters, and collectively they took their toll on Confederate military efforts. (*Photo of* Forest Rose *courtesy of the Public Library of Cincinnati and Hamilton County. Photo of* Cricket *courtesy of the U.S. Naval Historical Center*)

While Commander John Rodgers was purchasing commercial vessels to convert to gunboats, the Union was also contracting with James B. Eads of St. Louis for the construction of seven ironclad steamers to be specifically designed as river gunboats. Each vessel was 175 feet long with a flat bottom and shallow draft. Samuel M. Pook, who actually designed the new boats, armed each with ten 8-inch guns. He also located the vulnerable paddle wheels inboard and covered the sloping wooden sides with 2 1/2-inch armor. The new gunboats were commissioned *Mound City, Carondelet, Louisville, Pittsburg, Cairo, Cincinnati,* and *St. Louis* (later renamed *Baron DeKalb*). These seven ironclads saw more service than any class of gunboat on the western waters. Three of the boats, *Cairo, Cincinnati,* and *Baron DeKalb,* would eventually be sunk. Only the *Cairo* saw no action on Arkansas waters.

Probably the best known Union vessel and certainly the most unlucky boat to operate in Arkansas was the *Mound City.* On June 13, 1863, *Mound City,* along with *St. Louis* and *Lexington,* left Memphis and steamed toward the White River, with orders to protect troops and supplies that were being sent to aid General Samuel Ryan Curtis who was trying to seize Little Rock by marching overland from Missouri. On June 16, the squadron began steaming up the White River where they hoped to rendezvous with Curtis' forces near Jacksonport. However, the Confederates anticipated such a move and decided to challenge the flotilla at St. Charles. At a point where the river makes a meandering bend, the Confederates sank three steamboats in the channel. On a bluff overlooking these obstructions they sited two 32-pound rifled guns and four lighter weapons to sweep the channel. At 6 A.M. on June 17, the squadron, then anchored a few miles below St. Charles, got underway with *Mound City* in the lead. Captain Augustus Kilty steamed directly toward the sunken vessels, and soon a furious artillery battle began. Kilty continued to steam boldly onward until he had brought his vessel

within 600 yards of the Confederate batteries. Then disaster struck when a 32-pound shell shattered a casement and struck the boat's steam drum which promptly exploded. Almost immediately the vessel filled with live steam which badly scalded most of the crew. In their agony and fear, some of the men jumped overboard where they were killed by Confederate rifle fire.

One of the first officers to reach the disabled *Mound City* was the commander of the expedition, Lieutenant Wilson McGunnegle. He could hear the howling of the wounded as he arrived. Since most of the crew were casualties, McGunnegle immediately ordered sailors from the other boats to help man the *Mound City.* Discipline aboard the vessel had completely broken down, and soon many of the sailors were drunk. Some went about robbing the dying. "Rooms were broken open, trunks, carpet sacks, etc. pillaged, and their contents scattered around and destroyed. Watches of officers stolen, and quarreling, cursing, and rioting as well as robbing seemed to be the rule."[3] One sailor, scalded while standing by his gun, accidentally discharged the weapon into a nearby Union vessel. The shot severed a steamline, but fortunately no one was injured. Nearby, Captain Kilty lay badly burned while the master of the *Mound City,* Mr. Cyrenius Dominy, was so shocked by the disaster that he lost all control and had to be removed from the boat. That evening Union sailors buried fifty-five of *Mound City*'s dead. Only twenty-six of the 175-man crew escaped uninjured, and many of the wounded would linger in agony for weeks before finally dying of their wounds.

Soon *Mound City* was repaired and put back in service, but not before the survivors of her crew were exchanged with sailors from the gunboat *Tyler.* Eventually, *Mound City* and her new crew returned to the western flotilla and served throughout the remainder of the war. (*Photo courtesy of the U.S. Naval Historical Center*)

One of the largest naval vessels that operated on any Arkansas river was the *Blackhawk,* but the sternwheeler's 260-foot length, 45-foot beam, and 8-foot draft made her unsuitable for use except where the channels were deep and wide. Rear Admiral David D. Porter used *Blackhawk* as his flagship in the successful expedition against Arkansas Post. During the attack on January 11, 1863, *Blackhawk* stood off 800 yards from Fort Hindman and used her rifled artillery very effectively. However, the next day *Blackhawk* tried to close on the fort but the river was too narrow for her to maneuver. *Blackhawk* saw no further service on Arkansas rivers and spent most of her career serving as flagship of the Mississippi River Squadron. On April 22, 1865, she accidentally burned and sank three miles below Cairo, Illinois. Note the figure of her namesake, Blackhawk, chief of the Sac and Fox Indians, on the pilothouse. (*Photo courtesy of the Public Library of Cincinnati and Hamilton County*)

On April 17, 1862, Acting Master Cyrenius Dominy, of the gunboat *Mound City,* boarded the captured Confederate steamer *Red Rover* at her moorings near Island Number 10 in the Mississippi River. The 786-ton sidewheeler had recently been put out of service by shelling from the Federal fleet which had caused considerable damage to her deck and hull. The Federals took the steamer to St. Louis, where authorities converted her into the United States Navy's first hospital ship. The *Red Rover,* with her 300-ton icebox, nine water closets, laundry, kitchens, elevators, and ample deck space, was a perfect vessel for such a task. The Western Sanitary Association aided the conversion by providing $3,500 worth of medi-

cal supplies while the shipyard added an amputating room and covered the windows with gauze blinds to protect the patients from cinders and smoke. If necessary she could care for two hundred seamen at one time. Sisters of the Order of the Holy Cross, the pioneers of the Navy Nurse Corps, then came aboard, and *Red Rover* was ready to sail. One of her first duties would be to care for the scalded sailors from the *Mound City. Red Rover* remained with the western flotilla until the end of the war and cared for almost twenty-five hundred patients. During her career she made many trips to the port of Helena.(*Photo courtesy of the U.S. Naval Historical Center*)

In 1864, the crew of the *Signal* took time from their duties to pose for this photograph. The sudden need to create a riverine navy forced the Union to have to quickly acquire vessels and to locate crews to man them. Throughout the war, the Union had difficulty keeping the navy at full strength, and this problem was especially acute in the western flotilla. Initially, the navy had sent five hundred seamen from the East Coast to man the gunboats, but as one naval officer remarked, "this small number could do little more than leaven the lump with naval discipline." River steamboat men were available in fairly large numbers, but they were an independent breed of men who did not respond well to discipline.[4] They usually preferred to serve on commercial steamers. In the early months of the war, the most readily available source for manpower was the Union army. Soon Northern farm boys and city dwellers who had probably never seen a navigable river until they joined the service were being transferred to the boats. Sometimes army officers sent the men who caused them the most trouble, and General Grant himself recommended that those being held in the guard house for desertion and disorderly conduct be transferred to the gunboat service. Flag Officer Andrew H. Foote, in his desperation to obtain crews, reluctantly agreed to the proposal. (*Photo courtesy of the Arkansas History Commission*)

Freed slaves were another potential source of manpower. Throughout its history, the navy had accepted free blacks into the service, and on April 30, 1862, Secretary of the Navy Gideon Welles issued orders that former slaves be enlisted in the navy. Aboard the gunboats segregation was held to a minimum, and blacks were usually messed and quartered with white sailors. They responded well, and perhaps as many as 25 percent of the 118,000 men who served in the navy were blacks. A portion of the black crewmen aboard the *Signal* can be seen amidship on her main deck. She was anchored at De Valls Bluff when photographer R. H. White took this picture.

Like the gunboats themselves, these crews were a hodgepodge of seasoned sailors, blacks, riverboatmen, soldiers, and troublemakers. However, in time they became proficient in riverine warfare and helped contribute to the final Union victory. (*Photo courtesy of the Arkansas History Commission*)

The Union army relied on steamers such as the *Empire City, Des Arc, Pocahontas, Emma No. 2, Ella, Rowena,* and *Liberty No. 2* to move troops and supplies along the western waters. On their return trips, these vessels often hauled cotton and other agricultural products back to Northern cities. Since the boats were largely unprotected, they were favorite targets for Confederate guerillas even when they traveled with gunboats as escorts. The *Ella,* for example, was attacked between St. Charles and Clarendon on July 30, 1862. The rebels killed one soldier and wounded six others. Such attacks were common along the rivers. Occasionally, steamers like the *Empire City* had to face more serious attacks from Confederate artillery. On April 22, she was among six steamers that ran past the Vicksburg batteries. Confederates sank the steamer *Tigress* and totally disabled the *Empire City.* The latter vessel was repaired and later served on the White River. Underwater obstructions were also constant dangers. In April of 1863, *Rowena,* while steaming between Cairo and St. Louis, hit a snag and sank. She was later repaired and operated on the White River in 1865. Two years later, in October, 1867, she hit another snag near Helena and sank. Nor were the gunboats immune from stumps. On May 18, 1863, the *Signal* struck a stump on her starboard side which injured the executive offi-

cer and carried away parts of the bulkheads and cabin. These wooden vessels were also highly vulnerable to fire. On March 22, 1864, the *Des Arc* was moored at De Valls Bluff when the cotton in her hold caught fire. *Signal* towed *Des Arc* across the river to prevent the fire from spreading to the other steamers in the harbor. Soon the flames were out of control and the crew decided to scuttle the steamer to prevent her total loss. Unfortunately, the large amount of cotton in her hold prevented her from sinking rapidly. Finally *Signal* stood off from the steamer and fired six 32-pound shells into her hull. The *Des Arc* settled to the bottom. She was later raised and put back into service. After the war, *Des Arc* operated as a White River packet until she was dismantled in 1871. Without these ubiquitous transports, the Union army would not have been able to move so quickly the large quantities of troops and supplies that were needed to regain control of much of Arkansas. (*Photos courtesy of the Arkansas History Commission*)

Chapter 5

Little Rock

Following the attack upon Helena and the success of General Grant at Vicksburg, nothing stood in the way of a Federal assault on Little Rock. Grant returned troops to the command of Major General John M. Schofield, commander of the Department of Missouri. This made possible an expedition against the Arkansas capital. On July 31, 1863, Major General Frederick Steele arrived at Helena to undertake a drive on Little Rock.

Steele's command moved out of Helena in the middle of August. The march was slow and his twelve thousand troops quickly succumbed to the diseases rampant in eastern Arkansas. By the time his army reached Clarendon, over one thousand soldiers were too sick to continue. Steele initially hoped to create a base of operations at Clarendon, but found the position unsatisfactory. Instead, he moved about ten miles farther north on the White River to De Valls Bluff. Here he built fortifications, a hospital, and a depot to gather supplies. On August 22, the Federal cavalry began to reconnoiter the Confederate positions towards Little Rock. Steele's infantry began its westward advance on September 1.

Steele faced an army commanded by Major General Sterling Price. Price believed that he faced superior forces and attempted to consolidate all the troops available to him at Little Rock. Price ordered the construction of defenses on the north side of the Arkansas River to be used against Steele's army. He dispersed his columns on both sides, one brigade under Brigadier General D. M. Frost on the north, another under Helena native James C. Tappan on the south.

By September 7, Steele had reached the Arkansas River near Ashley's Mills. On that day, Steele's cavalry had a sharp skirmish that drove Confederate forces away from the river. As a result, Steele split his army, sending his cavalry across the river on a pontoon bridge. This maneuver completely flanked Confederate forces at Little Rock which were preparing to defend the city on the north bank of the Arkansas. Steele's two columns raced up both sides of the river facing little opposition. Only cavalry under John S. Marmaduke opposed the Union cavalry moving up the south bank.

Steele entered Little Rock on September 10. Price had ordered supplies evacuated from that city to Arkadelphia shortly after assuming command. This had not been completed, however, and the Union entry was so quick that Federal soldiers found that the Confederates had been unable to destroy what had to be left. While the railroad facility north of the river at Huntersville had been set on fire, Union soldiers were able to save two of the locomotives. At the old United States Arsenal, the entering Union troops found three thousand pounds of powder, cartridges, and five cannon that Price had been unable to remove and had failed to destroy, though six steamboats on the river were beyond saving. Steele's victory had been an expensive loss for General Price.

Confederate forces fell back all the way to Arkadelphia where they arrived on September 14. While Price reported an orderly withdrawal, units collapsed on the way to the southwest. Confederate troops would continue to operate in southwestern parts of the state, but much of the spirit had gone out of the men. Colonel Asa S. Morgan who was fleeing southward with the army from Little Rock wrote home to his wife, "The desertions here and the demoralization of his army [are] all that you have heard."[1] James Mitchell wrote at about the same time, "Our men have deserted dreadfully since we left L.R. . . . some of them the best soldiers we had—it is so in the whole army—they will not go South—I shall stick to them till the army 'goes up.' That may not be long."[2]

At the same time that Steele was marching on Little Rock, another Federal expedition drove Confederate Brigadier General William Steele from Fort Smith and the Indian Territory. Holding Fort Smith had been particularly essential, given the threat against Little Rock. Should it

fall, the Union army would have a supply line running from the Mississippi to Fort Gibson in the Indian Territory and would be able to act against Confederate forces anywhere along this line. Confederate general Steele had a difficult situation, for he was pressed in the Territory by General J. G. Blunt. After a battle at Backbone Mountain on September 1, Blunt's forces moved on into Fort Smith and established the western anchor of a line that cut the state in two.

Fortunately for the Confederates, once into Little Rock, Frederick Steele failed to pursue them. He chose instead to consolidate his position, sending troops to protect the Southern approaches to his headquarters by taking Pine Bluff. This respite allowed Price to regroup his dispirited army. By October, General Marmaduke was actually able to lead his cavalry in an aggressive attack upon Pine Bluff. Although Marmaduke failed, the attack indicated that Price had been able to stabilize the situation in his army and could offer a contest should Steele attempt to move farther south.

Rather than pursuing Price further, Steele appeared content to sit in Little Rock. Steele's dispatches indicate he believed the war in Arkansas all but won. He also considered his losses due to disease to stand in the way of a movement in strength into the southwest part of the state. The general abandoned military operations and, instead, worked to establish a loyal government in the state and to reinforce his own position. His enemies accused him of taking advantage of his situation at Little Rock to enjoy the good life.

The city of Little Rock was one place in Arkansas that the Federals liked. It was much more like the midwestern towns from which they came. Little Rock's square blocks and broad streets looked much more like home. The sidewalks were either paved or surfaced with sand and gravel so the mud that was so pervasive elsewhere in the state was not found in the city. The brick government buildings such as the State House and the Arsenal made the town seem more substantial than perhaps its 3,727 inhabitants warranted, and the residential areas, as well, carried that air of wealth and prosperity. The occupying forces quickly added to the city's appearance with the construction of warehouses and repair shops to service their needs. The military hospital at St. John's College was expanded. As an occupied city, Little Rock's economy boomed.

Among the factors contributing to Steele's optimistic assessment of conditions in Arkansas was the appearance of large numbers of former soldiers and citizens who came into Federal lines ready to bring the war to an end and swear an oath of allegiance. Among these was Brigadier General E. W. Gantt who issued an address asking the South to end the war and rejoin the Union. Many of these former Confederate soldiers were organized into Union regiments at this time. In addition, Steele allowed Arkansas to organize a free state government under Lincoln's plan of reconstruction.

By October, 1863, prominent Unionists in the city such as William M. Fishback had organized a Union movement. Under their sponsorship, a Union convention met at Little Rock the following January. Chaired by John McCoy of Newton County, the delegates rewrote the old constitution, abolishing slavery and declaring secession void. In addition they named Isaac Murphy as provisional governor and called for a statewide election on the second Monday in March. Lincoln approved of their actions and Steele gave his support. In the election, 12,403 Arkansans voted, about twenty percent of the number who had voted in 1860. The majority approved the new constitution and elected Murphy governor. While this government was never recognized by Congress, it continued to operate through the remainder of the war.

Like Helena, however, Little Rock soon became something of a trap. General Steele had a large army quartered in the city, and the surrounding countryside could not support it easily. As a result Steele began to build a supply line between the city and his old base at De Valls Bluff. While the Arkansas River provided the most direct route, the river was treacherous and could not always be counted on to have enough water for boats to reach him. Instead he took advantage of the already existing rail line to De Valls Bluff which he had managed to capture intact from the Confederates. The base at the Bluff was expanded, and rapid repairs were made to rolling stock and rails of the Memphis and Little Rock Railroad. The first trains began moving only ten days after the city's fall. In November, Steele also began rebuilding the telegraph between the city and Memphis.

By the end of 1863, Steele had established strong connections with Federal forces operating on the Mississippi, and he began to build up his strength. The move towards establishing a free state government was underway. Confederate forces appeared content to remain in southwestern Arkansas and leave his men unmolested. There was every reason to believe, if sitting in Steele's position, that the war in Arkansas had ended. His conclusion would prove, however, premature.

The fall of Vicksburg not only opened the Mississippi River, but it also released troops for use in the long delayed advance on Little Rock. The city seemed to be an ideal target for Union occupation since it was the capital of the Confederate government in Arkansas and it could serve as a logistical base for future advances into the southern counties. By 1863, the capital was feeling the effects of war. Flour, if it could be obtained at all, sold for $200 a barrel, and a pair of good leather boots cost $106. Confederate soldiers were common sights on the streets, but many were poorly clothed and "worn down with days of toil and marching."[3] A steady stream of these soldiers entered the hospitals. Despite the deteriorating conditions, anyone standing on the corner of Markham and Main Streets could not help feeling that Little Rock, with its brick buildings and gas lights, had not declined dramatically during the war. (*Photo courtesy of the J. N. Heiskell Historical Collection, UALR Archives*)

Private Jacob Boon was with the Third Iowa Cavalry on August 11, 1863, when he and six thousand other troopers moved out of Helena. They were the vanguard of General Frederick Steele's thirteen-thousand-man army that was advancing on Little Rock. Boon had joined the cavalry on September 10, 1861. On April 27, 1863, General John Marmaduke's men had captured Boon at White Water, Missouri, but he was released on parole in time to rejoin his company as it prepared to leave Helena. During the march, skirmishes with rebel cavalry were daily affairs, but these actions did little more than annoy the advancing Federals. The biggest nuisances to the troopers were the heat and mosquitos, but many soldiers found time to fish and swim in the rivers that they crossed. By September 9, most of the army was near the north bank of the Arkansas River. They would cross the next day. (*Photo courtesy of Roger Davis*)

Brigadier General John S. Marmaduke had studied at Yale and Harvard before he graduated from West Point in 1857. He joined the Missouri State Guard in 1861, and later fought at Shiloh, Prairie Grove, and Helena. In the summer of 1863, Marmaduke was second in command of a scratch force of one thousand three hundred cavalrymen who were trying to delay Steele, but his men could do little more than harass the advancing Federals. Since the Battle of Helena, Marmaduke had been feuding with his commander, Brigadier General Lucius M. Walker. On September 6, 1863, with Steele's cavalry almost within sight of the Arkansas River, Walker and Marmaduke were preparing to settle their differences; that morning the two met at Godfrey Le Fevre farm seven miles south of Little Rock to duel. They exchanged shots at fifteen paces, and Walker fell mortally wounded. The next day, most of Marmaduke's cavalry withdrew to the south bank of the river. (*Photo courtesy of the State Historical Society of Missouri*)

On September 10, 1863, Steele led the main column of his infantry directly toward the Confederate entrenchments on the north bank of the river, while another crossed south of Little Rock. At 2 P.M., the Federal column on the south bank reached Fourche Bayou, where the Confederates planned to make their final stand. Brigadier General James C. Tappan commanded one of the four Confederate brigades in the fight. Tappan, a Yale graduate and prominent Helena attorney, had helped raise the Thirteenth Arkansas Infantry. At Shiloh Church, he led the regiment in the brutal fighting around the Hornet's Nest. On November 5, 1862, he was promoted to brigadier general and transferred to Arkansas. For a short period of time, the rebels managed to halt the Union advance, but artillery fire, combined with a flanking attack, forced the Confederates to withdraw. The fighting cost the Federals about sixty casualties and sealed the fate of Little Rock. (*Photo courtesy of the UALR Archives*)

The Third Minnesota fought at Fourche Bayou, and because of its "efficiency and sound discipline," General Steele gave it the honor of leading the Union army into Little Rock.[4] Fifteen months earlier, the men of the Third Minnesota were not so lucky. On July 9, 1862, they were part of a brigade stationed in Murfreesboro, Tennessee, when General Nathan Bedford Forrest suddenly pounced on the unsuspecting garrison and captured it. After being paroled, the Third was transferred back to its home state, where it spent most of its time fighting the Sioux Indians. It finally returned to the war in time to participate in the capture of Vicksburg, Mississippi. The regiment is shown on parade in 1864 in front of the capitol at Little Rock. Shortly after the fall of Little Rock, B. T. Simmons, a soldier from the Third Minnesota, wrote his sister that they were quartered in the State House and "having a big time of it, we walk on fine carpets, sit in large cushioned chairs, and sleep on spring beds."[5] (*Photo courtesy of the J. N. Heiskell Historical Collection, UALR Archives*)

The Little Rock expedition had cost the Union army only 137 casualties, and the occupation of the capital had been easily accomplished. However, Steele was now deep within rebel territory and he could not remain where he was without establishing a secure, logistical system to supply his troops. According to army regulations, his men would need to be issued 20 tons of rations daily, and his 24,000 horses and mules would consume 120 tons of fodder per day. In addition, the army would need medical supplies, tents, uniforms, powder, shoes, and all the other accoutrements that kept the soldiers fighting. Some of these supplies could be had locally, but most would have to be shipped from Northern depots far up the Mississippi River. Since the Arkansas River was a treacherous stream below Little Rock, Steele could not depend on that route. Instead, he had to rely on the riverport at De Valls Bluff. There, the steamers could unload their supplies into government warehouses such as these. (*Photos courtesy of the Arkansas History Commission and the National Archives*)

The supplies at De Valls Bluff were loaded on the United States Military Railroad and transported fifty miles to another complex of warehouses at Huntersville on the north shore of the Arkansas River, immediately opposite Little Rock. (*Photo courtesy of the National Archives*)

The supplies were then ferried across the Arkansas River to Little Rock. (*Photo courtesy of the National Archives*)

The fifty-mile stretch of railroad was the most vulnerable part of Steele's line of communications, and it became a favorite target for marauding rebels. It required constant patrolling to protect the road, and that work fell to troopers like Private Clark Keyes and Sergeant Walter Wood of Company I, Third Michigan Cavalry. The Third was now protecting the trains, but the men also had experience in destroying them. In August, 1863, the regiment helped burn sixty locomotives and almost five hundred cars at Granada, Mississippi. Confederate raiders usually struck without warning. On July 6, they exploded a mine which derailed a locomotive and killed its crew. Nine days later, they fired into a train and wounded two soldiers. On July 17, and again on the 24th, they tore out small sections of the track. Most of the time, the rebels escaped before the patrols could catch them, but on July 31, they were not so fortunate. A cavalry detail surprised some raiders on the prairie and captured a few prisoners. These patrols were tedious operations, and discipline was often difficult to maintain. On July 4, 1863, some of the troopers from the Third Michigan broke into a warehouse in De Valls Bluff and carried off twelve barrels of beer. Two of the men filled their canteens and drowned while trying to swim the river. (*Photo courtesy of the Arkansas History Commission*)

The rapid build-up of men and material in Little Rock placed a heavy strain on the available building space in the capital city. The State House, prison, and U.S. Arsenal provided some immediate room, but there were not nearly enough public structures for the needs of thirteen thousand soldiers. However, Little Rock did have a number of good private commercial buildings such as these facilities on Main Street (the northeast corner of Second and Main streets), and many were used by the military. (*Photo courtesy of the National Archives*)

By the summer of 1864, the army had occupied most of the available buildings and had begun constructing its own facilities. Timber was easily available and the army began running its own sawmill. Soon thousands of board feet of rough lumber were available for construction. (*Photo courtesy of the National Archives*)

Most of the warehouses were simple structures like these four buildings on Markham
Street which were made of rough hewn lumber and cypress shingles. Each was 138 feet
long and 38 feet wide. The two-story building served as the commissary subsistence
office for the army. (*Photo courtesy of the National Archives*)

Fires were a constant threat to these
wooden buildings, and the army took some
rudimentary precautions to protect them. If
a roof fire started, soldiers would remove
the ladders from the walls, climb up them,
and dump the barrels of water on the flames.
(*Photo courtesy of the National Archives*)

The final link between Steele's long logistical tail and the fighting men were the ubiquitous army wagons. These heavy lumbering machines were designed for hard use, and an old soldier ruefully noted that "as a pleasure carriage . . . they were not considered a success." He added that "no harder vehicle can be found to take a ride in than an army wagon."[6] It is difficult to know exactly how many wagons Steele's army had when he occupied Little Rock, but his 13,000-man army would have been authorized to have approximately 370 wagons and about 50 artillery caissons. By March 31, 1864, his command had reached 16,189, which would have added at least 120 more wagons to his command. (*Photo courtesy of the Arkansas History Commission*)

Early in the war, horses were generally used to pull wagons, but as the demand for cavalry mounts grew, they were gradually replaced by six-team army mules. The mules were better able to withstand hard use, poor food, and neglect, but they had several distinct disadvantages. Most of the animals were unnerved by gunfire and "preferred to do military duty in the safe rear." Therefore, they were largely useless for artillery units and for hauling munitions to the battlefield. Mules were also stubborn, unpredictable, and prone to kick without warning. "He cannot be trusted," wrote one soldier, "even when appearing honest and affectionate. His reputation as a kicker is worldwide. He was the mugwump of the service. The mule that will not kick is a curiosity."[7] (*Photos courtesy of the National Archives*)

Civilians such as this group in front of a warehouse in Little Rock were sometimes used by the army as both laborers and teamsters. The mule drivers spoke "a sort of gibberish" to the animals as they pulled on the reins. Many also carried long whips that they liked to crack over the animal's head as they hollered in "mule tongue." A good teamster could launch into an almost unlimited "stock of profanity with which he greeted the sensitive ears of his muleship when the latter was stubborn." As a last resort, teamsters were known to physically attack the animals. One veteran remembered seeing a black mule-driver get flattened by an unexpected kick from one of his animals. The teamster slowly picked himself up, walked to his wagon, "took out a stake the size of his arm" and delivered the mule "a stunning blow on the head" which knocked him to the ground. The animal lay there for a minute "then rose, shook his head, a truce was declared, and driver and mule were at peace and understood each other."[8] (*Photo courtesy of the National Archives*)

136

One of the largest complexes constructed in Little Rock consisted of the repair shops located on a 300-square foot block of ground between Rock, Cumberland, Cherry, and Mulberry streets. The shops' primary function was to keep hundreds of wagons in serviceable condition. Workers in the building on the right were capable of fabricating the entire wooden frame, tongue, and boxes, while the carpenters who worked in the building on the left usually built or repaired smaller wooden parts. The building in the foreground housed the paint, harness, and sail makers' shops. (*Photo courtesy of the National Archives*)

The final building on the repair shop quadrangle was the blacksmith's shop. Inside were eighteen forges where men worked building or repairing metal parts for the wagons. It also contained another thirteen smaller forges the smiths used to make horseshoes for the teams. (*Photo courtesy of the National Archives*)

Steele also had to find quarters for his troops, and the army seized at least thirteen homes to house high-ranking officers and their respective staffs. The ordinary soldiers' billets were less impressive, and most men such as those of the Twenty-eighth Wisconsin Infantry had to build their own. This cabin was probably constructed in December of 1864. Captain Thomas N. Stevens of Company C, Twenty-eighth Wisconsin, wrote his wife that the "ground is wet & cold, & it is our only floor, it is rather uncomfortable. The chimney to my shanty is built of stones & old bricks about four feet up, then finished off with sticks. The window sash is of soldier's manufacture, as is all the rest of the house & trimmings. Wish you could look in and see us."[9] (*Photo courtesy of the J. N. Heiskell Historical Collection, UALR Archives*)

A few soldiers were more fortunate than the Twenty-eighth Wisconsin since they were housed in barracks that the Quartermaster's Department had built. The men quartered in these eight barracks on the U.S. Arsenal grounds could enjoy such niceties as front porches, glass windows, good stoves, plank floors, and well-ventilated roofs which provided some relief during the summer. (*Photo courtesy of the Arkansas History Commission*)

Like most armies throughout history, the rear echelon soldiers have usually managed to live better than their companions in the line regiments. The employees of the Quartermaster's Department occupied these barracks on Cherry Street. The 44 x 20-foot buildings contained complete kitchen facilities as well as a clearstory for better light and ventilation. (*Photo courtesy of the National Archives*)

Soldiers in the Civil War spent most of their time doing menial tasks rather than fighting. Musician A. F. Sperry of the Thirty-third Iowa remembered that in Little Rock he could look forward to "drills, and parades, inspections, and reviews" that "took about all the time that picket and fatigue-duty left unoccupied."[10] Still, the garrison duty in Little Rock did offer some amusements for the men. Some visited the library of the Christian Commission or occasionally enjoyed a play at the theater, but other soldiers' tastes leaned more toward whiskey and cards. As soon as the paymaster arrived, the proprietors of the billiard parlor and the Icy Shades Saloon on Markham Street were busily liberating soldiers of their greenbacks. (*Photo courtesy of the J. N. Heiskell Historical Collection, UALR Archives*)

Chapter 6

Medicine and Disease in Civil War Arkansas

Few of the soldiers who served in the Civil War completed their enlistments without spending some time in military hospitals. Between 1861 and 1866, the Union medical services handled a staggering 6,029,560 admissions relating to illness in all theaters of operations. The hot, wet southern environment, poor sanitary conditions in the camps, polluted water, and a diet of beans, salt meat, and biscuits were all major culprits. These conditions explain why diarrhea, dysentery, malaria, typhoid fever, bronchitis, and pneumonia accounted for well over half the hospital admissions. In this atmosphere, the average soldier was likely to be sick at least twice per year, and it was not unusual for ten percent of all Union troops to be absent due to illness. In addition to these statistics, it was also recorded that one soldier in twenty who entered the hospital because of disease died there.

Figures compiled from Arkansas hospital returns for the period July 1, 1863, to June 30, 1865, indicate that the state was the most un-

healthy command in the army. During that period, the mean monthly strength was 28,462 men, but those actually present for duty usually numbered about 19,000. In those same two years, Union hospitals recorded 178,194 admissions for illness, and only 4,457 cases of wounds, accidents, and injuries. Almost without exception, disease rather than wounds accounted for most deaths in regiments. The Thirty-third Iowa Infantry, which served almost exclusively in Arkansas, is fairly typical. From an original muster of almost a thousand men, the unit lost sixty-eight soldiers in combat, while two hundred and sixteen others died from disease.

Reliable statistics for Confederate soldiers are more difficult to obtain, but most experts agree that because of the chronic shortage of medical supplies, food, and clothing in the Southern armies, their mortality rates were even higher than those of the Union armies.

In the rural South, few young men had been exposed to communicable diseases, and when they first arrived in camp, sickness usually swept through the ranks of raw recruits. W. L. Gammage, a surgeon with the Fourth Arkansas Infantry, wrote that his regiment had only been in camp a few days when measles, "that terrible scourge of all armies," made its appearance.[1] During the next sixty-six days, hundreds of soldiers contacted the disease and at least thirty-three died. Private J. P. Blessington of Walker's Texas Division suffered a similar experience while encamped near Austin, Arkansas, where "dysentery and fevers" filled the hospitals and killed more than fifteen hundred men during the winter of 1862–1863. Blessington believed that much of the sickness came from impure drinking water.[2]

Soldiers stationed along the marshy rivers of eastern Arkansas were especially susceptible to malaria and various lung infections. Assistant Surgeon Junius Bragg told his wife that Arkansas Post was a "vile place. It is so unhealthy here in the summer season, that nothing can live except mosquitoes. I am credibly informed by the oldest inhabitant that the snakes have chills." He added that so many of the soldiers had jaundice that the command looked like a tribe of Indians.[3]

In the early days of the war, the Confederates tried to bury their dead with military honors. When Private Frank B. Williams, Company F, Fourth Arkansas Infantry, died of congestive fever, the body was placed on a wagon and escorted with muffled drums to his grave. However, such niceties soon disappeared. By 1863, so many soldiers were dying in Little Rock that they were usually buried in long trenches. After passing through the burying ground one soldier remarked that "the sight was sickening; bones protruded through the thin covering of earth and the stench was almost unendurable."[4] Under such conditions, Confederate units usually lost fifty percent of their strength per year, which meant that a regiment carrying 1,000 men on its rosters on January 1, 1863, would be able to field only about 250 men by January 1, 1865. These attrition rates due to disease were so high that one authority has concluded that after the capture of Little Rock, the war degenerated into an eighteen-month stalemate, primarily because neither side had enough healthy soldiers to efficiently conduct offensive warfare.

In contrast, admissions because of battlefield wounds accounted for less than seven percent of those who entered hospitals, and these losses were not large enough to affect significantly the military situation in Arkansas. However, these injured soldiers suffered horrible agonies because of the terrible damage that Civil War weapons could do to human flesh. If a bullet or shell fragment smashed a bone in the extremities, doctors usually had to amputate the limb. Wounds in the chest or abdomen were more difficult to treat, and even if the soldier survived the operation, he was likely to die within a few days from internal hemorrhaging or infection.

Since most soldiers were wounded in large numbers in short periods of fighting, neither Confederate nor Union medical corps had the capacity to move them to hospitals. After the Battle of Pea Ridge, for example, Surgeon Gammage remained behind on the field to treat the thirty-six wounded men of his regiment. For the first two days, the men had nothing to eat except a few scraps of food that could be scrounged from the haversacks of the dead. Finally, he managed to kill a hog and to prepare hot food for the soldiers. Twenty-five days later, Gammage was still in the field, but ten of his wounded had died. One other soldier had had his leg amputated, and Gammage had removed the hand of a Sergeant Spear. Six more men finally recovered, but had to be discharged for medical reasons. The list of injuries included smashed thighs, broken arms, head wounds, and facial lacerations.

If a soldier could get to a hospital after a battle, he found conditions there to be not much better than in the field. Shortly after the Battle of Prairie Grove, William Baxter visited one of the Union hospitals in Fayetteville where the floor was "so thickly covered with mangled and bleeding men" that he had difficulty avoiding stepping on them. Baxter recorded that "some were mortally wounded, the life fast escaping through a ghastly hole in the breast; the limbs of others were shattered and useless, the faces of others so disfigured as to seem scarcely human." His heart sickened when he saw the surgeons "carving and sawing the limbs of men like butchers in the shambles."[5]

By 1865, thousands of young men who had marched off to war in Arkansas were either dead or disabled. Most had not been victims of enemy fire. Instead they had succumbed to disease, the real killer of armies since time immemorial. The reality of death and suffering had also destroyed the youthful innocence and enthusiasm of these men. They would continue to fight, but many soldiers could sympathize with Privates William H. and John Shibley of the Twenty-second Arkansas Infantry, who in the summer of 1863 wrote their parents: "We are greatly in hopes that the time through the good providence of God may not be far off when this unholy war may end and we may return home in peace."[6]

Confederate authorities established the first large hospital in Little Rock on the grounds of St. John's College, a military academy that had begun operating in 1859. The three-story structure was soon filled to capacity, and by February, 1862, the Confederates were operating at least twenty other smaller facilities in the city. On March 15, 1863, Surgeon Junius Bragg wrote his wife that he was about to be transferred to St. John's College. "The Post Surgeon has his clutches on me," he wrote, "and I am of the opinion he will keep me as long as he can." He added that a number of the medical staff in the hospital "have a knack for drinking all the whiskey they can lay hands on."[7] (*Photo courtesy of the J. N. Heiskell Historical Collection, UALR Archives*)

When the Federal army occupied Helena in June 1862, authorities began to convert residences such as General Thomas Hindman's home into military hospitals. The town proved to be very unhealthy, and the hospitals were soon overflowing with soldiers. As the young men died, they were buried in the beautiful hills that surrounded the town. Conditions in Helena had not improved by 1864, when the inspector of posts reported that the health of the troops in Helena was "very bad indeed," and that the town was the "most deadly place on the river."[8] (*Photo courtesy of the Arkansas History Commission*)

Sergeant Leander Stillwell of Company D, Sixty-first Illinois Infantry, became ill with malaria shortly after his arrival in Helena on July 31, 1863. Because he had "seen so many of the boys loaded into ambulances . . . and hauled off to hospitals . . . who never returned," he resisted going on sick call as long as possible. Stillwell and the rest of the sick men from his division were placed in walled tents and attended by other soldiers who were too weak for any other work. At night, bayonets were stuck in the ground with a lighted candle in the socket. Most of the candles burned out by midnight and the sick remained unattended in the darkness until morning. Those who could take food usually received a watery barley or rice soup and a piece of hardtack. Stillwell remained in the hospital eight days where, as he noted, "aside from men dying all around me both day and night, nothing important happened."[9] (*Photo courtesy of the UALR Archives*)

The big logistical base at De Valls Bluff became the major medical complex for the men stationed along the lower White River, and this particular structure probably housed only officers. To the north of De Valls Bluff lay the little village of Clarendon, which eventually lent its name to the rampant fevers that preyed on the soldiers. Many men believed that "the real, genuine 'Clarendon Shake' is to any ordinary chills and fever about as a bulldog is to a pet poodle."[10] (*Photo courtesy of the National Archives*)

Many of the enlisted men who succumbed to the "Clarendon shake" and other maladies were treated in these buildings. Continued illness in De Valls Bluff so debilitated the garrison's strength that it often interfered with the army's operations. On July 17, 1864, Brigadier C. C. Andrews explained that his defenses were not complete because it required a great amount of labor and that "it is no small job either to dig the graves that are now required."[11] He added that two small regiments had already buried twelve men within the last twenty-four hours. After eighteen months' duty at De Valls Bluff, the Third Minnesota had 150 deaths from fever, and the governor of Minnesota pleaded with military authorities to transfer the survivors to another location where they might at least "have an opportunity to die at the post of honor."[12] His plea went unheeded and the unit remained there until the war ended. (*Photo courtesy of the National Archives*)

When the Union army occupied Little Rock, they found that the retreating Confederates had left behind about fourteen hundred sick rebels. Most of these men were housed in St. John's College and in the two large two-story wards that the Confederates had constructed on the college grounds. However, even these new facilities were not large enough to care for all the sick from both armies. By the end of the war, Union authorities had added eleven more single-story wards to the complex. (*Photo courtesy of the National Archives*)

Junius Bragg, a recent graduate of the Louisiana State Medical College in New Orleans, joined the Confederate army in May, 1861, and held a variety of surgical posts in Arkansas. Southern physicians were as well-trained as their Northern counterparts, but there were fewer of them, and the Confederacy was woefully short of medical supplies. Southern surgeons rarely had adequate stocks of opium, morphine, ether, or chloroform to use during surgical procedures and usually had to rely on preparing the men with liberal doses of whiskey. Fortunately, quinine was usually available for malaria, and Bragg treated himself with the following concoction: "I commenced taking quinine . . . every two hours until I had a half dozen safely lodged under my vest. Then to cap the climax, I took a teaspoonful of gunpowder dissolved in . . . a tin cup of vinegar. . . . I took, also the benefit of a good dose of Blue Mass."[13] Bragg survived his cure and surrendered with General E. Kirby Smith in Texas on June 2, 1865. (*Photo courtesy of the Public Library of Camden and Ouachita County, Arkansas*)

On August 17, 1861, Lieutenant John N. McCollum of Pike County joined the Fourth Arkansas Infantry. The regiment went on to fight in most of the major campaigns in the western theater, but because of illness Mc-Collum never saw any action. On November 10, 1862, he asked to resign from the service because of "long continued ill health and the firm belief that the service will kill me if I continue it." The examining surgeon provided a report of symptoms common to many Civil War soldiers—"ascites, the result of long continued disease of the bowels; he is also laboring under great emaciation and extreme debility."[14] McCollum's resignation was accepted. (*Photo courtesy of Mike Polston*)

151

Private Steven K. Porter was in Company C, Dobbins' Arkansas Cavalry, when he "took sick" at Cotton Plant. His family rented a wagon to carry Porter and another ill soldier back to their homes in Independence County where they could be nursed back to health. He arrived home on Monday and died the following Sunday, on December 18, 1862. Soldiers like Porter knew that they might die in combat, but as in the case of almost ten thousand other Arkansas Confederate soldiers, their killers were not Yankee shells, but disease. Thirty-year-old Private Porter left behind a wife and three children. (*Photo courtesy of Mrs. Ralph Porter*)

At the Battle of Pea Ridge, Captain Robert P. Mathews of Phelps' Independent Missouri Battalion was severely wounded when a Confederate minié ball smashed through his upper chest and lodged against his right shoulder blade. Sixty-two percent of the Union soldiers who received these types of wounds died, but Mathews was lucky. Physicians treated him on the battlefield and then moved him to Springfield, Missouri, where on April 27, 1862, he was discharged as being unfit for further duty. (*Photo courtesy of the Washington County Historical Society*)

Andrew Patton mustered into the service on December 12, 1863, and eventually became chief surgeon for the Sixtieth U.S. Colored Infantry. Many black soldiers spent much of their time in unhealthy garrisons in the delta and suffered disease rates that consistently exceeded most white regiments. Patton's regiment, for example, fought in only one battle, where it lost 11 men, but from its original muster of 1,153 soldiers, 332 died from disease. (*Photo courtesy of the Iowa State Historical Department.*)

Chapter 7

War Gives Way to Guerilla Action: Camden to the End of the War

On March 23, 1864, General Frederick Steele's army marched out of Little Rock, its intention being to join up with another army under General Nathaniel Banks marching northward in Louisiana against Confederate forces under E. Kirby Smith. The Red River campaign was part of the general offensive begun by Federal forces in the spring of 1864 and was designed to place pressure on all Confederate lines, hopefully, to destroy one of the last remaining Confederate armies. With Steele marched some ten thousand men along with twenty-five pieces of artillery. His plan was to link up with another five thousand men commanded by Brigadier General John M. Thayer who was marching from Fort Smith to Arkadelphia. Once united, the combined force would drive towards Shreveport through Camden.

As Steele's men moved towards the southwest they thought they were moving into a wilderness. Every farm was deserted and few human beings were seen, nor any hogs or cattle. The least developed part of the state before the war, it was now almost desolate. In addition, Confederate cavalry under the commands of Marmaduke and Cabell harassed Steele's movements along the way. Despite delays, he had brilliantly pulled the Confederate armies out of his main direction of march with a feinted drive toward Washington, Arkansas, the state's Confederate capital. When Price moved from his trenches at Camden to stop Steele at Prairie d'Ane, the Federals paraded uncontested into that heavily fortified town of over two thousand inhabitants on the Ouachita River on April 15.

Although he had moved with ease to Camden, Steele found himself deep in enemy territory and uncertain of the situation with Banks. In fact, Banks had been repulsed by Kirby Smith at the Battle of Mansfield and Smith was now marching with his troops to join Price against Steele. Unsure of the situation, Steele ordered all of his units to concentrate at Camden and quickly prepared for a siege. His hopes of establishing a supply line via the Ouachita River were dashed when the river went down and his gunboats and supply ships could not move upriver. At that point, Steele put his men on short rations and set up two flour mills to grind the grains seized along the way so that his men could be fed until an alternate supply line could be set up with the Arkansas River at Pine Bluff.

The first indication of Steele's isolation came when his supply lines began to be attacked. Disasters at Poison Spring and Marks' Mills practically cut his line. On April 18, Confederates attacked a foraging party sent out by Steele at Poison Spring. The party included troops of the Eighteenth Iowa, two squadrons of cavalry, two pieces of artillery, and the Second Kansas Colored. With them were large numbers of slaves fleeing to freedom. Steele lost over two hundred wagons, along with five hundred men. The Second Kansas suffered particularly badly, losing over half of its members when Confederate attackers refused to accept their surrender.

Steele pulled farther back into Camden and ordered an end to foraging. Fortunately, a supply train broke through to Steele on April 20. As Shelby moved closer, however, Steele was unsure of what he should do. When Captain F. Heineman asked General Frederick Salomon what Steele intended to do, Salomon replied, "Steele knows that he is a West Pointer, and doesn't appear to know anything about Arkansas, where he is or what he is doing. Damn these regulars! They map out battles on paper, draw their salaries and—smoke cigars. The worst of it is they always keep clear of the fire line, which bars the luck of getting them shot out of the way!"[1] When Heineman asked Salomon further what they would do if they could not link up with Banks, the general replied, "Then we'll run and fight and run. What else can be done?"[2]

On April 24, Steele's situation deteriorated further when his supply train, returning to Pine Bluff for more supplies, was ambushed at Marks' Mills and captured. Benjamin Pearson noted that Confederates singled out blacks for special treatment. He wrote, "they shot down our colored servents & teamsters & others what were following to get from bondage, as they would shoot sheep dogs."[3] After Marks' Mills, the Federal position was untenable, and Steele ordered a retreat back to Little Rock on April 26, 1864. The weather was bad and the columns of troops raced desperately northward along muddy roads, hoping to prevent being cut off before they reached the Saline River. Captain Heinemann of Salomon's staff, by now convinced that Steele was incompetent, expressed concern with what he considered the general's plan. "Save our artillery and baggage, run like whiteheads for the Saline bottom, cut through anything that puts itself in our way, and with the river at our back, the bogs at our flanks, face about and fight for our lives. Will we make this point? That is the question."[4]

Steele retreated towards Little Rock while E. Kirby Smith pursued him. At daylight on April 30, Federal and Confederate troops arrived at a ford known as Jenkins' Ferry. Through the day, Confederate troops threw themselves against the lines of the retreating Federals, but failed to break them. By the end of the day, Steele had managed to draw his army north of the Ouachita and to relative safety. On the morning of May 1, Steele burned his wagons, eight hundred of them, his medical stores, clothing, regimental and company papers, and headed home. Private John P. Wright of the Twenty-ninth Iowa wrote of the retreat, "Country level, heavy timbered. Desperate roads, no improvements, perfect wilderness . . . Mud that no mule's leg would fathom."[5]

Coming back into Little Rock, Steele's army was in disarray. Nonetheless, it re-formed its ranks outside the city. The Second Kansas Colored Infantry, credited with taking a Confederate battery at Jenkins' Ferry and three stands of Confederate colors, led the defeated army back into the strongly fortified lines around the state capital.

Steele's defeat caused a panic among loyalists

in the state. Governor Isaac Murphy wrote to President Lincoln, "The army and the people are discouraged. Confidence in the commander is lost. Go where you will in the army or among the citizens you hear the same despairing tone. The feeling is that unless strong reinforcements are soon here and more energy displayed by the military authorities Arkansas will be again in the hands of the rebels."[6]

The defeat at Camden changed the entire situation in Arkansas. Steele had been optimistic the previous year. Now the Confederates were given another chance. While the Union army withdrew into fortified positions in Little Rock, Pine Bluff, De Valls Bluff, Fort Smith, Fayetteville, and Helena, the Confederates roamed about the countryside at will. The war deteriorated into a swirling conflict of cavalry and guerillas. Steele's army stayed as much as possible within its lines, although attempting to protect its lines of communication—the railroad to De Valls Bluff, the White River to the rail line, and the Arkansas River from Little Rock to Fort Smith. Small units were spread along all of these lines to fight bushwhackers. Steele's tactics were so costly, however, that they led to a temporary decision to abandon Fort Smith, a decision which only political pressure prevented from occurring, and these factors led to—perhaps ultimately resulted in—his replacement by General Joseph J. Reynolds in December, 1864.

Efforts to control the supply lines occupied much of the Federals' time as Confederate raiders attacked communication lines throughout the state. The year 1864 marked a Confederate resurgence. Perhaps the most optimistic operation was along the Mississippi where rebel raiders attacked Union plantations around Helena and also attempted, unsuccessfully, to close the Mississippi at Chicot County. In the interior, Confederates placed guns on the Arkansas River and forced a fleet trying to go to Little Rock to return to De Valls Bluff. Later the same month, General Joseph Shelby's cavalry accomplished an unusual feat when they attacked and seized Gunboat 26, the *Queen City*, on White River. Shelby's operations along White River between De Valls Bluff and the Mississippi so threatened Union operations that a force of five thousand men and the gunboat *Tyler* were sent to clear them out. At the same time, Confederates carried on frequent raids upon the military railroad between the De Valls Bluff depot and Little Rock.

If regular forces were not bad enough, Union forces encountered extensive action by irregulars who waged guerilla warfare against them. In the vicinity of St. Charles, a unit led by a man named Brown operated against the Federals until in September a cavalry scout, looking for men who had shot into boats, encountered and killed him. Also near St. Charles, Doctor John A. Morgan operated against Federal foraging parties in the fall of 1864. Morgan's career ended when he was captured by the Eighteenth Illinois Mounted Infantry in December, 1864. A witness who saw Morgan in captivity and on his way to a northern prison described this raider as "about 5 feet 10 inches high [,] long black hair, and a piercing and restless black eye. Well educated, and talkative. He is a smart but dangerous man."[7] In the vicinity of Des Arc, the twenty-one year old Texan, "Yellow Doc, the Ranger," "Doc Rayburn," or Howel A. Rayburn ran his guerilla operations. In northwestern Arkansas, bushwhackers roamed at will through the mountains, hiding in the forests of the area.

Union forces had no permanent solution to this new type of warfare. The Third Arkansas Cavalry, U.S. Volunteers, is a typical example of the units spread out along the lines of communication in a fruitless effort against the elusive raiders. Some argued that Steele was reluctant to take any type of decisive action and preferred to ride out what now appeared to be the inevitable Union victory in Little Rock. One Kansas officer, Joseph Trego, wrote, "I have heard no reasons assigned for such mismanagement except that the officers . . . prefer remaining in the city and

Steele don't like to incur their displeasure by ordering them away."[8]

Under Reynolds, Union forces continued their actions. The state penitentiary, appropriated for holding bushwhackers and guerillas, filled up. Little changed, however, and the Civil War in Arkansas wound down in a stalemate with neither side able to win a victory. Confederates controlled the countryside; the Federals controlled the cities. As late as April 8, 1865, Confederate forces were able to move unmolested into the town of Dover, burn it, and escape without fear of Federal intervention.

The stalemate in Arkansas ultimately ended due to the occurrence of events elsewhere. On April 9, 1865, Confederate armies in Virginia under General Lee surrendered. The other major Southern army, that under Joseph Johnston, was being surrounded in North Carolina. On April 14, Major General Reynolds at Little Rock asked General Fagan, as Confederate commander the District of Arkansas, to surrender his forces. Fagan refused, but turned over his command to General Thomas P. Dockery and left the state. While officers and officials debated surrendering, apparently many men decided to end the war on their own and deserted. On June 2, General Kirby Smith finally surrendered to the Federals, after which, on June 3, Dockery surrendered his men and Arkansas, although Fagan returned to surrender again on June 14. Across the state, Confederate soldiers ended their fight. Some would flee to Mexico and South America; most went home. For all, however, the Civil War in Arkansas was over.

The decisive General Frederick Steele, once having secured Little Rock, concluded that his command could not further pursue the Confederates into southwestern Arkansas. Sickness among his men and supply problems provided him with his reasoning. Steele was not allowed to sit at Little Rock, however. That autumn, 1864, General Nathaniel Banks, at New Orleans, planned a spring offensive against Shreveport, Louisiana, and wanted Steele to stage an attack through southwestern Arkansas against Shreveport from the North. Steele tried to stay out of this action, requesting that his army be used to stage a demonstration only. The new commander of the armies of the United States, Lieutenant General Ulysses S. Grant, ordered Steele to make a real movement instead. Grant was anxious to destroy Confederate forces west of the Mississippi so that troops could be diverted from the Trans-Mississippi area to the eastern theater. A decisive battle against the last major Confederate army in this region at Shreveport would free enough men for what Grant hoped would be a strike at Mobile in conjunction with Sherman's move into the South from Chattanooga. A reluctant Steele left Little Rock on March 23, 1864. Over half of his cavalry was dismounted. The cavalry with horses, the artillery, and other transportation used horses in poor condition. In a letter to General William T. Sherman, Steele complained, "This department is the last to be served."[9] (*Photos courtesy of the Arkansas History Commission and Special Collections, David Mullins Library, University of Arkansas at Fayetteville*)

First Lieutenant W. W. Granger, adjutant of the Third Missouri Cavalry Volunteers, rode out of Little Rock with his unit on Steele's march into southwest Arkansas. Steele used his cavalry units to screen the movement of his army, to scout out the main body of the army of Confederate General Sterling Price, and to forage supplies from the surrounding countryside. Steele ran into Confederate cavalry under John S. Marmaduke on the first day out of Little Rock, but the Union army had little difficulty pushing aside the smaller Confederate units. On April 9, Steele finally encountered more stubborn resistance at Prairie d'Ane where Price had concentrated his army to prevent the Union capture of the Confederate state capital at Washington. The Third Missouri, returning from a foraging expedition, rejoined Steele on April 11, just in time to be thrown into line on the Union right in an attack upon Price's position on the western edge of the prairie. At dark the Union forces drove across the prairie and forced the Confederates into a rapid retreat, but the darkness and rain ended the pursuit. After having returned to their previous positions in camp, Union forces found the Confederates had returned to theirs as well. On the morning of the 12th, the two armies were in the same places they had been prior to the previous day's fighting. One member of the Third Missouri wrote of this return, "Verily, thought we, they are an impudent set of rascals."[10] Price would not fight on the 12th, however, and moved back towards Washington again, hoping to draw Steele onto ground more favorable to the Confederates. Steele, with his supply line back to Little Rock exposed to cavalry raids, beset with rumors that the Red River campaign was not faring well, and confronting Price's main army, decided, instead of pursuing, to shift his force to Camden on the Ouachita River in order to use that stream as his source of supply and communication. (*Photo courtesy of the UALR Archives*)

Steele was in an exposed position as he moved into Camden. On April 8 and 9 in battles at Mansfield and Pleasant Hill, General Nathaniel Banks' Union army had been forced to retreat from before Shreveport down the Red River. General E. Kirby Smith, commander of the Confederate Trans-Mississippi Department, now turned his attention and his men northward towards Steele, whom he hoped to trap away from his base of supply. As part of this operation, Smith ordered Price's two cavalry divisions to attack and cut off all of Steele's supply trains. In addition to picking up Federal foragers and stragglers, the Confederate cavalry began to make Steele's position untenable. On April 18, a force under Brigadier General William L. Cabell overran a Federal foraging party of about nine hundred infantry and three hundred cavalry at Poison Spring, seizing nearly two hundred wagons filled with Steele's badly needed provisions. A decisive engagement occurred, however, on April 25 when Brigadier General James F. Fagan, shown here, and his entire cavalry division swept down on Steele's supply train at Marks' Mills. Over two hundred wagons were lost, and their escort of nearly two thousand men was captured. (*Photo courtesy of the UALR Archives*)

162

Orlando P. Sala of West Point, Iowa, was eighteen years old when he enlisted in the First Iowa Cavalry in August, 1862. He fought at the battle of Prairie Grove in December, 1862. In the spring of 1864, he and his unit were with Steele at Camden where they reenlisted as a veteran regiment. Because of this reenlistment, Steele was forced to furlough them. The unit left Camden shortly after the general's supply train that was to be destroyed at Marks' Mills. The First Iowa marched up on the battle and were heavily engaged. Rather than boarding steamers at Pine Bluff destined for Iowa, the unit found itself fighting its way back towards Camden. Most of the unit rejoined Steele, Sala among them. The battle at Marks' Mills convinced the Union commander that he would have to retreat. On the evening of April 25, Steele polled his commanders and all agreed. The next morning the Union army left Camden and began a tortuous march back over the path that it had taken to the southwest. (*Photo courtesy of Roger Davis*)

Brigadier General Samuel A. Rice, commander of Steele's First Brigade in Brigadier General Frederick Salomon's Division found himself in charge of the rear guard as the Union army retreated toward Little Rock. Because Steele had moved swiftly out of Camden, Confederate forces were having to rush forward over bad ground in an effort to cut off the fleeing Federals. They finally received an opportunity when the Union army halted in the bottoms of the Saline River to erect a pontoon bridge and cross this last major barrier to their escape. The Confederates found a brilliant enemy in Rice who personally led the regiments protecting the main army as it crossed the river. In the battle at Jenkins' Ferry on April 30, the Federal rear guard effectively used the muddy grounds of the river bottom in combination with their own fire power to stop the Confederates. At one point, Rice took the lead of the Second Kansas Colored and Twenty-ninth Iowa in a counter-attack upon the Confederates. In that attack, Rice was wounded in the right foot and subsequently lost it, but his leadership had helped to prevent the destruction of Steele's army as it lay on the south side of the Saline. Steele cited both Rice and his commander Salomon as officers "of Superior Merit."[11] (*Photo courtesy of Bill Rasp*)

164

Hugh McCollum of Camden was with the Confederate army that was pursuing Steele. McCollum had been in the Confederate service since May, 1861, when he joined the First Arkansas Infantry. He was severely wounded at Shiloh in April, 1862, and sent home to Camden. McCollum had not taken long to recover before, in June 1862, he joined the Thirty-third or Grinsted's regiment. As they marched after Steele, the regiment was on its way back from the Confederate victory at Pleasant Hill, Louisiana, ready to drive the Federals out of Arkansas. As part of James C. Tappan's Brigade, the Thirty-third was one of the first units to run into the Federal rear guard at Jenkins' Ferry. The Thirty-third was held in reserve while Tappan ordered two of his consolidated units forward, the Nineteenth and Twenty-fourth, and the Twenty-seventh and Thirty-eighth. Making no headway, Tappan threw the Thirty-third against the Federals. Lined up less than one hundred and fifty yards from the Federals, the Confederates drew a withering fire. Junius N. Bragg, regimental surgeon, wrote of the battle, "There was nothing of the romance of war or battle. . . . Two hundred-twenty men could not last long before an army corps. After a few trial minutes the regiment fell back in disorder leaving ninety-two wounded and killed."[12] Among those killed were Colonel H. L. Grinsted and Hugh Mc-Collum, dead twenty-five days after his twenty-second birthday. (*Photos courtesy of the Public Library of Camden and Ouachita County, Arkansas*)

Colonel H. L. Grinsted

Captain Jacob Wythe Walker, son of prominent Unionist Judge David Walker of Washington County, was with the Thirty-fourth Arkansas on the field at Jenkins' Ferry. His unit was part of Hawthorne's Brigade, a unit composed of the remnants of whatever units could be scraped up in Arkansas in the spring of 1864. As Tappan's units were destroyed, Hawthorne's came up on the scene and was thrown into action. General Thomas J. Churchill reported, "the firing, now incessant, was terrific, and the struggle was desperate beyond description."[13] Despite all their effort, they were forced from the field by Federal fire. Walker was carried from the field badly wounded and then taken to nearby Tulip, where Walker's father and brother nursed him, but he died on May 21. (*Photo courtesy of the Washington County Historical Society*)

The battle and carnage at Jenkins' Ferry effectively blunted Smith's efforts at cutting Steele off from Little Rock. Except for some cavalry skirmishes, the main body of Steele's army effected their escape. On the first day back, Sergeant P. B. Greaves, Company A, First Iowa Cavalry, went to a photographer at Little Rock to have his picture made. On the back he wrote, "Taken on our return from the Red River expedition to Little Rock, taken before washing & c. Was gone 46 days, traveled 486 miles, had 40 fights & skirmishes, was on picket duty 28 times, lived on dry corn three days & nothing two days had to retreat for the first time."[14] Greaves' spirit, like that of his commander, seemed taken aback by the Camden disaster. After it, Union attention would shift to eastern theaters of operation, and the Union effort in Arkansas would become one of holding on against increasingly audacious Confederate marauders. (*Photo courtesy of the UALR Archives*)

On May 7, 1864, the Union forces in Arkansas became part of the Military Division of West Mississippi under the command of Major General Edward R. S. Canby. Because of the failure of the Red River and Camden expeditions, General of the Armies Ulysses S. Grant had decided to restrict operations west of the Mississippi and concentrate his forces in Virginia and with Sherman in Tennessee. Canby was instructed to "limit the remainder of his command to such operations as might be necessary to hold the positions and lines of communications he then occupied."[15] In Arkansas that thin line ran from Fort Smith on the Arkansas River along the border with the Indian Territory, down river to Little Rock, overland to De

Valls Bluff by the Little Rock and Memphis Railroad, then down the White River to the Mississippi. The eastern anchor of the Federal line was at Helena. This photograph is of a Federal encampment on the parade grounds at Fort Smith that was taken at about this time. The command of General Thayer at Fort Smith would remain virtually isolated during the rest of the war, and Thayer would complain about the shakiness of his position. Nearly abandoned in December, 1864, the orders of General Grant caused its reoccupation the following January. Almost forgotten, Fort Smith remained the western outpost of Union forces in Arkansas through the rest of the war. (*Photo courtesy of the UALR Archives*)

Captain John T. Blake, Company I, Sixth Kansas Cavalry, was typical of the men charged with protecting Fort Smith during the latter years of the war. The Sixth had fought at Prairie Grove and participated in General Blunt's later advance against General Hindman's beaten army at Van Buren. In November, 1863, the regiment moved to Fort Smith. Elements of the unit marched with General Thayer and joined Steele on the Camden expedition. The unit then regrouped at Fort Smith where it remained until the end of the war. Service on the frontier was dangerous for these men. On July 27, 1864, the Sixth Kansas was serving as an outpost unit at Mansard Prairie, about six miles from Fort Smith. Rebel raiders badly mauled the unit, capturing some 120 of the troopers. Captain Blake was not among the prisoners, and he managed to survive the war and be mustered out with the unit. (*Photo courtesy of the UALR Archives*)

General Frederick Steele took very literally Grant's orders to engage the enemy only to protect the Arkansas River line. Steele pulled his men as close to the river as possible. Rather than protecting agricultural lands around the river, he became more reliant upon his line of supply from the Mississippi River. His command became the object of increasing complaints from the men of his army. One went so far as to accuse the general of refusing military action in order to enjoy the pleasures of Little Rock. In fact most of his men seemed to enjoy the same pleasures, and the Union army in Arkansas began to lose its fighting edge. This photograph shows Steele and his staff in December, 1864, when he was being relieved by General Joseph J. Reynolds. This picture is actually a composite, produced in Little Rock on the occasion of Steele's departure. (*Photo courtesy of the Arkansas Historical Association*)

Steele's continued occupation of Little Rock actually appears to have been of some benefit to the town. The presence of the army with its pay and the spending of money on military installations brought a prosperity to the town that it had not experienced before, certainly not since pre-war days. This photograph looks westward along one of the town's main streets, Markham. The Arkansas River can be seen to the right. Also visible are several buildings constructed for the military in 1864. These buildings, freshly whitewashed, included both a warehouse and barracks along Markham. (*Photo courtesy of the National Archives*)

Among the many buildings constructed at Little Rock during the continued Union occupation was a forage house capable of storing 9,300 square feet of goods built on the city's Cherry Street, between Ferry and Rector. To the west of the downtown, the government built a stable complex. The low buildings to the back of the complex were the stables, capable of housing nearly a thousand horses. The building with a number 2 drawn on it was housing for teamsters. Building number 3 was the mess and forage house for this facility. (*Photos courtesy of the National Archives*)

171

In addition to its payroll, the army brought to Little Rock a wide variety of entertainments that for the soldier in the field must have made the town seem like a very desirable place to be. This photograph shows a typical military band of the time, with bells of the brass instruments pointed over the shoulders of the musicians, serenading the staff at Steele's headquarters in the Ashley mansion. (*Photo courtesy of the Arkansas History Commission*)

The order to hold the Arkansas River line also led to the creation of a permanent post and a build-up of facilities at De Valls Bluff on the eastern terminus of the Little Rock and Memphis Railroad. These photographs show part of the Federal facilities occupied during this period. One photograph is a view of the quartermaster stables at the re-mount camp outside of town. The other photograph is an unidentified building, possibly headquarters for the post commander. (*Photo of stables courtesy of the National Archives. Other photo courtesy of the Arkansas History Commission*)

Quartermaster stables

As at Little Rock, operations out of a permanent garrison allowed the soldiers to add various amenities to their lives. While regulations passed in July, 1862, had eliminated bands below the brigade level, the Third Michigan Cavalry which was stationed at De Valls Bluff in the winter of 1864–1865 reconstituted its band. This photograph shows the Third Michigan's band as it posed for a photographer, very probably White, at its barracks at De Valls Bluff. Like other military bands, this one probably spent much of its time playing for the men in camp. (*Photo courtesy of the Arkansas History Commission*)

Confederate General Joseph O. Shelby was in a position in the spring of 1864 to make Steele's orders to hold the Arkansas River a very difficult assignment. On May 5, Shelby received orders to march to the rear of Steele's army, establish himself in the White River area, and disrupt Steele's lines of communication along White River and the Little Rock and Memphis Railroad. On May 13, his command crossed the Arkansas River at Dardanelle and began three months of preying upon Steele's command, three months that severely threatened the Federal hold on central Arkansas. (*Photo courtesy of the Missouri Historical Society*)

The first Federals to feel the presence of Shelby along the Arkansas River were Colonel Abraham H. Ryan's Third Arkansas Cavalry (Union). They were stationed at Lewisburg engaged in the dirty business of fighting guerillas and bushwhackers. When his outpost was captured at Dardanelle, Ryan was faced with a bad problem. Outnumbered, he had no option but to pull his troops out of Lewisburg, although he thwarted Shelby's efforts to capture supplies at his post by putting most of his materials in houses infested with smallpox. (*Photos courtesy of the Arkansas History Commission and the UALR Archives*)

Colonel Abraham H. Ryan

Major H. Van Houten

Shelby arrived at his base of operations on the White River unmolested. He immediately began recruiting new troops, rounding up former Confederates who had deserted, and putting some sort of order into the numerous guerilla bands that had been fighting in the area. He made his presence felt by the Federals on June 24, 1864, when his command staged an attack on the tinclad *Queen City*. Lying at anchor in the White River off the town of Clarendon, the boat and its crew were not aware of Shelby's presence. He had dismounted his men and brought four pieces of artillery within fifty feet of the vessel. At four in the morning, his men opened fire on the boat, and its surprised crew surrendered. With other gun-

boats in the vicinity, Shelby acted quickly. He removed a 24-pounder and a 12-pounder from the *Queen City,* then opened her magazines and blew it to pieces. Emboldened by his success, Shelby decided to wait and attack the advancing gunboats. Within the hour, *Tyler, Fawn,* and *Naumkeag* came round a bend and both sides opened fire. Soon the fire from the flotilla overwhelmed Shelby's field artillery and his two newly captured pieces. When *Tyler* moved within fifty yards of the shore and began firing canister into his troops, Shelby withdrew from the contest. Nonetheless, he had the distinction of having captured the only Union military vessel taken in Arkansas. (*Photo courtesy of the Arkansas History Commission*)

Captain Doc Rayburn, also referred to as Rayborne, was typical of the guerillas encountered by Federal forces as the war drifted towards an end. Rayburn was a lieutenant in Parson's Texas cavalry when it moved across Arkansas to join Price in Mississippi in 1862. At Des Arc, the unit waited for steamboats on the White River to move them to Mississippi, but Rayburn contracted some sort of fever. He remained behind, but at some time recruited a company of men that operated behind Federal lines after 1863. Although Rayburn was supposedly commissioned as a captain, his command is never referred to as a part of the regular Confederate army. One of the few references to his actions came after a party of sixty of his men, dressed in Federal uniforms, surprised and mauled a party of the Eleventh Missouri Cavalry on July 28, 1864. When Shelby's cavalry moved out of the state with Price in August, 1864, Rayburn remained in Arkansas, in the bottoms of the Little Red River in the vicinity of West Point. He was never captured, and local tradition holds that he was shot after the war by a disgruntled Confederate soldier. He is supposedly buried near Des Arc, but the place of his grave has been forgotten. (*Photo courtesy of Lawrence T. Jones*)

The story of Captain Jacob G. Becton of Crabtree's Cavalry or the Forty-sixth Arkansas Mounted Infantry was typical of those of many of the soldiers who surrendered or were captured in Arkansas in the spring of 1865. Becton had enlisted in the Seventeenth Arkansas Mounted Infantry at Des Arc on February 15, 1862. In the spring of 1863 the Seventeenth was merged with Colonel Jordan E. Cravens' Twenty-first Arkansas Infantry and the unit was thrown into the defense of Vicksburg. On May 16, it fought at Champion's Hill, and Becton was captured. Becton was sent to Johnson's Island in Ohio until he was exchanged. He returned to Arkansas and joined the Forty-sixth, a unit formed from the men who had surrendered at Vicksburg and Port Hudson. For the summer of 1864, the Forty-sixth served in eastern Arkansas where it was with Dobbins in his attack on Lamb's Plantation near Helena in August. Becton and his unit then went with Sterling Price on his raid into Missouri in August, 1864. After that raid's failure, the Forty-sixth did not fall back to Texas with the rest of Price's army but moved into eastern Arkansas where it remained through the rest of the war, raiding Federal supply lines and operating almost as guerillas. The war finally ended for Becton on May 3, 1865, when he was captured by the Ninth Kansas Cavalry in Prairie County. Sent first to De Valls Bluff, Becton was then transferred to the military prison at Little Rock where he remained until released upon taking an oath of allegiance on May 7. (*Photo courtesy of the UALR Archives*)

General Archibald Dobbins, from Helena prior to the war, was one of Shelby's commanders in eastern Arkansas during the summer of 1864. While Shelby's main force operated against the railroad in central Arkansas, Dobbins and his command were sent to the Mississippi River in the vicinity of the Federal post at Helena. Dobbins had orders to put pressure on that post and also to stage raids on government-run plantations along the Mississippi. In his actions, Dobbins proved very successful, and his activities created severe problems for the Federals along the river. (*Photo courtesy of the University of Arkansas at Fayetteville Special Collections*)

The Sixtieth U.S. Colored Volunteers, composed of men of the First Iowa African Descent, was one of the units stationed at Helena. These three photographs show several of the unit's white officers. The pictures were probably made shortly after the unit was mustered in during December, 1863. The rolls of the unit showed 1,153 men who served during the war. Of these, only 11 were killed in battle, but 332 died of disease. The Sixtieth was engaged in only one battle, but that one would be a costly engagement with Dobbins' cavalry at Big Creek, west of Helena. In an operation to discover Dobbins' strength, components of the regiment were engaged in action on July 25, 1864. Dobbins possessed overwhelming strength and quickly overran the Federals. The unit fought its way back into its lines at Helena, but lost 11 of the 360 who had been on the patrol. Among those killed were the regiment's colonel, its surgeon, one captain, and its adjutant, Major Theodore W. Pratt (shown here with beard). (*Photos courtesy of the Arkansas History Commission*)

2ᵈ Lt Kisse   Cap.t   1ᵃˢᵗ Lt Brusle

Brigadier General Napoleon Bonaparte Buford was in command of the Federal garrison at Helena. Despite the pressure of Dobbins and other nearby Confederate commands, Buford could do little more than let them cut up his outposts. Facing what he thought were six thousand men, Buford did not have enough soldiers to do more than protect the town of Helena. On August 1, 1864, Dobbins staged a major attack on the Federal plantations, driving off the black workers, the stock, and killing all those people who resisted. Shelby would report that Dobbins' men had killed "75 mongrel soldiers, negroes, and Yankee schoolmasters, imported to teach the young ideas how to shoot."[16] Buford moved against the raiders with his two infantry regiments, although he could only muster four hundred men; the rest of the unit was sick. Despite his superior strength, Dobbins had no desire to fight infantry, and his cavalry left Buford's foot soldiers behind. The photograph of Buford and his wife was made at Helena on August 6, five days after the attack. (*Photo courtesy of the Arkansas History Commission*)

Unable to stop the raids of Shelby and his lieutenants, Steele found himself fighting to keep his lines of supply open. All of his available regiments, including the Twelfth Michigan Infantry whose officers are shown here, were thrown onto the rail line between Little Rock and De Valls Bluff. The Twelfth Michigan was engaged in skirmishes from late in May into August. On August 24, they fought back in a large raid against the road near Brownsville. Shelby took 577 prisoners, destroyed 10 miles of track, 3,000 bales of hay and 20 "hay machines," and razed 5 Federal forts. At the moment that it looked darkest for Steele's command, however, Shelby withdrew. His August 24th attack was actually intended to draw attention away from General Sterling Price's movement of the main Confederate army in Arkansas north of the Arkansas River as a prelude to his expedition into Missouri. By August 30, Shelby and his men were with Price on their way north and the Twelfth Michigan was thrown into a hasty, but unsuccessful, pursuit of the Missouri raiders. (*Photo courtesy of Bill Rasp*)

Colonel William F. Slemons, commander of the Second Arkansas Cavalry, was one of the officers marching with Price into Missouri. Slemons had been a member of the Arkansas secession convention, then had enlisted as a lieutenant in Ragland's cavalry. He had become colonel of the Second Arkansas in May, 1862, and led the unit in western Mississippi in 1862 and 1863. The Second had been moved west of the Mississippi early in 1864 and as part of Fagan's cavalry division had fought at Marks' Mills and Jenkins' Ferry. Started with great hopes, Price's expedition into Missouri proved to be a high-water mark for the Confederacy in the Trans-Mississippi. With his supply lines extended and facing an overwhelming force, Price began to fall back late in October, 1864. The retreat turned into a rout. In a fight at Marais des Cygnes, Kansas, on October 25, 1864, Slemons' unit was pressed by Federal attackers. The colonel's horse was shot and fell upon him, trapping him under it. With one hundred of his men, Slemons was captured and sent to the Federal prison at Johnson's Island near Sandusky, Ohio. In February, 1865, he was moved to Rock Island Prison, Illinois, where this photograph was made. Like many other members of the ill-fated raid by Price, Slemons would spend the rest of the war in Federal hands. The capture of Slemons and so many others left the Confederacy with no force capable of carrying on traditional military operations in Arkansas. Price and those men he could bring back moved into northeastern Texas. (*Photo courtesy of the Arkansas History Commission*)

The Confederate defeat in Missouri and the movement of the regular Confederate troops out of much of the state ushered in a particularly violent time in the history of the war in Arkansas. While regular operations ceased, vicious guerilla activity would continue up until the end of the war. The old state prison at Little Rock, used as a military prison and as barracks throughout the war, became the scene of more and more executions as Federal forces brought in captured guerillas and bushwhackers. (*Photo courtesy of the National Archives*)

Following Price's raid, many Union units were pulled out of Arkansas and put into operations against Mobile or transferred elsewhere to be used against the Confederate forces in the East. Only a thin line of Union troops was left, many of them members of Union regiments recruited in Arkansas, both white and black. Captain George W. Moore of the Second Arkansas Cavalry Union Volunteers was with one such regiment. Largely recruited in the vicinity of Batesville after Curtis had moved through the area in 1862, the Second Arkansas was stationed almost until the end of the war in northwestern Arkansas, protecting the area between Fayetteville, Arkansas, and Pilot Knob, Missouri. Typical of their operations was a scout from Springfield, Missouri, into Huntsville and Yellville between November 11 and 21, 1864. The four-hundred-mile trip saw none of the command lost, but they captured 22 prisoners, 19 horses, 5 mules, 7 revolvers, 4 McClellan saddles, about $600.00 of Confederate scrip, and $3.45 U.S. money. The entire trip, however, was a running fight with remnants of Price's army and bushwhackers. (*Photo courtesy of the Arkansas History Commission*)

Aaron Harvey, shown here with the side drum, was a slave from Mississippi who was brought to Helena with one of the cotton raiding parties. At Helena he enlisted in Company F, Fifty-seventh U.S. Colored Infantry. Like most other black regiments, the Fifty-seventh spent much of the war providing support to supply lines after being mustered in on December 2, 1863. The Fifty-seventh was first assigned to guard duty at the Post of Arkansas, then sent to Little Rock where it would spend most of the rest of the war helping to defend the Memphis and Little Rock Railroad. A small detachment was assigned as engineers and bridge train guard on Steele's expedition into southwestern Arkansas in the spring of 1864. This photograph of the color party of the Fifty-seventh was probably made some time after the war when the unit was mustered out at Little Rock on December 31, 1866. (*Photo courtesy of the UALR Archives*)

In the end, guerilla action could not stop the war from coming to its conclusion. The defeat of regular forces on all fronts made it impossible for the Confederacy to continue the fight. It reflects the nature of the last months of the war in Arkansas, however, that the last major Confederate force surrendered in the state, the command of Brigadier General M. Jeff Thompson, had been acting practically as a guerilla unit since it had fled from Missouri with Price. Thompson had moved into the bottoms of the White and Little Red rivers and continued to harass Federal supply lines after the main Confederate army had moved back into Texas. In May, 1865, a Federal expedition went into Thompson's area to inform him of the surrenders of Lee and Johnston and to demand the surrender of his forces. Thompson was not sure of his authority to surrender a force "not surrounded or in danger of immediate capture,"[17] but did so after consulting with his commanders. He agreed to the surrender on May 11. Lieutenant Colonel C. W. Davis, who received the surrender of Thompson's men at Wittsburg and Jacksonport, reported that Thompson had more men than the Federals had estimated—7,454 in all. They had little left to them, however, with which to make war. They surrendered five hundred guns, between three hundred and four hundred canoes, no public animals, and they had no food. Davis noted, "They seemed highly pleased at the surrender, and said that all they wanted now was to be allowed to live at home."[18] With Thompson's surrender, the war was over in Arkansas. (*Photo courtesy of the UALR Archives*)

189

Chapter 8

After the War

When the war ended, those Arkansans who returned home faced a new world. The fighting had stopped, but the damage had to be repaired. For each returning soldier, Confederate or Union, the postwar years presented numerous challenges. Economic life had to be restored. The state's government had to be restored to a moral relationship with the nation. The psychological trauma of the war had to be healed. Peace could return only when all of these problems had been dealt with.

Many of the young men who had marched to war in 1861 would not be available to help restore the Union in 1865. Over seventy-four thousand men from Arkansas fought in the Union or Confederate armies, a figure which constituted nearly sixty-eight percent of the male populace old enough to serve. The war had devastated that group. Some sixty thousand men entered the Confederate forces from Arkansas; and, if they suffered the same percentage of casualties as the other Southern armies, some 5,460 of them

would have died in battle or from wounds received in battle, and some 9,540 from disease and accidents. The Union army enlisted 8,289 white troops in the state, and 1,713 men of these troops died in service. Approximately 6,000 black troops came from the state, and the death rate among these soldiers was probably comparable. Literally, a quarter of all soldiers who served in the armies from Arkansas died.

Those who did return found an economy that was in disarray. The slave work force was now free, and whites and blacks would have to develop new arrangements among themselves. The fields had been untended. Business had been left unmanaged. As if these problems were not enough, the price of cotton soared in the first several years after the war, then plummeted. By 1870, the number of acres being cultivated by Arkansas farmers had dropped over six percent below the levels farmed in 1860. The value of the same farms declined over sixty-five percent. Every crop showed less production. Only in manufacturing did the 1860s show hope, for there the number of establishments, workers, wages, and value of products increased.

Despite the weakness of agriculture, reconstructing the state's economy proved the least difficult of the problems faced by veterans. By 1880, farmers had surpassed antebellum cotton production. The completion of major railroads linking the state to Missouri, Tennessee, and Texas signaled a revival of commerce. Businessmen and farmers were already beginning to talk about a "New South" with industry and cities as well as farms, and Arkansas would stride alongside the rest of the South in this progress.

Political reconstruction was a more difficult problem to solve. Arkansans had been divided over the question of secession in 1861. They had continued their internal divisions during the war. Now, Confederate and Union Arkansans emerged from the war with deep suspicions of each other. Hostility and hatred generated by the war remained a major barrier to the accomplishment of a real end to it. Into the 1870s, politics reflected the split in wartime loyalties.

Unionists now controlled the state government. Isaac Murphy had been elected governor by Union loyalists in 1864, and he presided over the state government during the critical years immediately following the war's end. Unionist control was continued when voters selected Powell Clayton, the former federal commander of the post at Pine Bluff, as governor in 1868, and Elisha Baxter, colonel of the Fourth Arkansas Mounted Infantry (Union), as governor in 1872. Arkansas Unionists were not a majority, however, even when black voting began in 1868, and their control over the government depended largely on the demoralization and then disfranchisement of many of their Confederate opponents. In March, 1873, an amendment to the state constitution restored the voting rights of all former Confederates, and made possible an end to Unionist control and the rise of Confederates to power through the Democratic party.

The old Confederates were ready for power. Many of Arkansas' Confederate leaders had fled the state after the surrender either because they feared the vengeance of the victorious Unionists or because they did not want to live in the postwar world. Their withdrawal was only for a short time, however. General Thomas C. Hindman had taken refuge in Mexico, but was back and embroiled in state politics by 1868. Robert W. Johnson, Confederate congressman, attempted to go to Mexico, but returned to Little Rock and became deeply involved in reconstruction politics. Albert Pike, Confederate commissioner to the Indians, went to Canada. Though he never again lived in Arkansas, he came back to the United States, and from his homes in Memphis and Washington, he remained an important force in the state's politics.

In 1874, the conflict between Unionists and Confederates ended when the Democrats achieved permanent control over the state government, and the former Confederates returned to power. Thereafter, a candidate's having fought for the lost cause would be the basis for his political preference. Unionists simply gave up their battle, finding no means of gaining political power. Until 1893, every governor of the state had served in the Confederacy. Augustus H. Garland, governor from 1874 to 1877, served in the Confederate Congress; William R. Miller, 1877–1881, had held the position of Confederate state auditor; Thomas J. Churchill, 1881–1883, had been a major general; James H. Berry, 1883–1885, lost a leg at Corinth; Simon P. Hughes, 1885–1889, had been a lieutenant colonel; and James P. Eagle, 1889–1893, had also served as a lieutenant colonel. While extensive biographical information is not available on other public offices, it is clear that Confederates dominated them from state to county level. Of thirty of the most prominent Confederate leaders from Arkansas, most regained, during this period, a large portion of their political prestige, and ultimately their economic power.

With the return of the Confederates to power, those who had supported the South in secession began to fit themselves back into the Union by vindicating their position. For Unionists, the fact of victory had validated the righteousness of their cause, but for defeated secessionists, there was no such easy justification. Southerners needed a rationale that would explain the correctness of their action in 1861 and why they had failed. The "myth of the Lost Cause" provided that rationale and made possible the reintegration of the Confederates into national society.

The premise of this myth was simple. The South had not fought to protect slavery but to defend its constitutional rights. Therefore, the cause had been just. Fighting for a righteous cause, the Confederate soldier lost not because he lacked a proper reason to fight or because of personal inferiority but because he was overwhelmed by the numerical and material superiority of the North. Even before the war ended, Arkansans were beginning to contribute to the idea of the "Lost Cause." In 1864, for example, W. L. Gammage of the Fourth Arkansas Infantry reminded the readers of his book, *The Camp, the Bivouac, and the Battlefield,* that throughout the South "little green hillocks cover the bones of her brave boys who fell in battle, martyrs of the cause of Southern independence."[1] In the decades following the war, other ex-Confederate Arkansans wrote about their war experiences and each added to the illusion of a physically defeated, but spiritually unconquered Southland. Perhaps none expressed this sentiment better than veteran Joe M. Scott when he wrote:

The 22nd of July, 1865, I landed home, accepting the results of the four years' service as a Confederate soldier, conquered but not convinced. I believed then as I believe now, the principles we fought for was right, that of state's rights and local self-government, and I have no patience with a man that offers an excuse for being a Confederate soldier. . . . I think if there is any one on earth that should be honored it is the true ex-Confederate, who entered the army without gun, tents or blankets, and I believe when history becomes impartial the records will show the Confederate soldiers to be the best fighters on earth. It is well known we fought a superior force from first to finish, yet we were victorious in many hard-fought battles.[2]

As the years passed and the war faded into history, it was inevitable that the old soldiers would forget the tribulations that they had endured and would begin to look back on their experience with fond memories. Various groups of ex-Confederates became active in all the Southern states. Many of these groups came together in 1889 to form the United Confederate Veterans, whose goal was "to unite in a general federation all associations of Confederate veterans."[3] The UCV intended to use its official organ, *The Confederate Veteran,* and a system of local clubs called camps to promote "social, literary, historical, and benevolent" activities for its membership.[4] Soon former Confederates were busily writing of their experiences for the *Veteran.* Sprinkled throughout the issues of the journal are many accounts of Arkansas soldiers. At the local level, the camps provided an opportunity for the veterans to meet informally. By 1904, one hundred camps were active in Arkansas alone.

Southern women also contributed to the "Lost Cause" myth through the United Daughters of the Confederacy, which organized in 1894 "to instruct and instill into the descendents of the people of the South a proper respect for the pride in the glorious war history."[5] The first Arkansas chapter of the UDC began in Hope in 1896, and within a year seven other chapters had been formed. In addition to the UDC and the UCV, other organizations such as the Ex-Confederate Association of Arkansas and the United Sons of Confederate Veterans were active in the state. Throughout the last decade of the nineteenth century and the earlier years of the twentieth, these societies worked diligently to care for the aging veterans and to memorialize the Southern cause. The Ex-Confederate Association took the lead in establishing the Arkansas

Confederate Home and in lobbying through the General Assembly a series of pension bills for ex-Confederate veterans and their widows. Meanwhile the UDC became involved in saving historical sites such as Confederate cemeteries, battlefields, and the Old State House. In addition, they raised funds to build monuments to the Confederacy throughout the state. By the first decade of the twentieth century, UDC-inspired monuments dotted the state to remind Arkansans of the patriotic sacrifice of the South. These monuments with glowing tributes such as "TRUTH CRUSHED TO EARTH SHALL RISE AGAIN," "LEST WE FORGET," and "FURLED BUT NOT FORGOTTEN" still stand as stark reminders of the enduring legacy of the Civil War and the myth of the Lost Cause.[6]

Sadly, those Arkansans who had remained loyal to the victorious Union could not share in the myth. Even though groups such as the Grand Army of the Republic, the Union equivalent of the UCV, had their camps in Arkansas, they exerted no influence in the shaping of the Southern mystique. Surely Thomas Boles, speaking before the twenty-first annual encampment of the Arkansas Department of the Grand Army of the Republic, echoed the feelings of many loyal Arkansans when he declared:

With peace, liberty, prosperity and happiness blessing all our land and people, why is it we are continually having dinned into our ears something about the "Lost Cause"? In the name of common sense and reason we would ask what is it they have lost in their defeat. They tell us that slavery was not the only cause of the war, and yet it was the only loss they sustained by it. And still they bemoan their "lost cause." Now it would seem that a decent respect for mankind would require of them to make known what their "Lost Cause" is, or stop complaining about it.[7]

The Civil War had left deep scars among Southerners, but in time those wounds began to heal. Much of that healing had occurred because the Union had not carried out a punitive policy against the defeated Confederacy, and Southerners were allowed to rationalize away their rebellion by creating the ideal of the Lost Cause. Symbolic of the healing of these wounds was an event at Little Rock on May 30, 1913. On that day, old soldiers from both the blue and the gray formed ranks with the khaki uniformed regulars of the United States Army in front of the Old State House to march in the Memorial Day parade. Their destination was the National Cemetery, where the federal government had recently acquired the adjacent land known as the Confederate Burial Ground. The wall that had separated the two cemeteries had been demolished. The graves of six thousand Union soldiers and seven hundred Confederates were strewn with flowers. Each headstone flew a tiny United States flag. The old soldiers milled around among the graves, "and shook hands, not over a bloody chasm, but in an open space with no line to mark the burial places of the two armies."[8] While the healing was not yet complete, the bitterness had largely been replaced with nostalgia for an era long past. Surely as Bruce Catton observed, civil wars have had worse endings.

194

Following the war, the Federal army maintained its presence in Little Rock throughout the Reconstruction period. A garrison was established at the old Arsenal. These photographs, made from the original glass plates, show what may have been part of a regiment, a military band, and one piece of artillery at evening colors at the Arsenal. (*Photos courtesy of the Arkansas History Commission*)

Elisha Baxter was the last Republican governor of Arkansas until the election of Winthrop Rockefeller. In the 1872 election, Baxter led the regular Republicans against Joseph Brooks and the insurgents. Baxter won the election, but allegations of widespread voter fraud continued to plague his administration. Baxter's position among Republicans was further compromised when he began to support many of the policies of the politically banished Democrats. The problems eventually led to armed conflict between the supporters of Brooks and Baxter. The short-lived war left at least fifty Arkansans dead or wounded. (*Photo courtesy of the Arkansas History Commission*)

198

Governor James H. Berry

William Fishback

After 1873, ex-rebels were enfranchised, and service with the Confederacy became an essential qualification for every governor for the next twenty years. In 1882, Arkansans elected James H. Berry as governor. Berry had served with the Sixteenth Arkansas Infantry at Pea Ridge and had later lost his leg in the Battle of Corinth, Mississippi. Like most of the Democratic leadership, Berry was a fiscal conservative, but he did support equal justice for blacks. Berry was popular enough to have won a second term, but he declined to run because he could not live on the parsimonious salary that the General Assembly authorized for the Governor's Office. Four years later, Arkansans broke with their twenty-year tradition of electing ex-Confederates and selected William Fishback as governor. In 1864, Fishback had been instrumental in raising a regiment of Arkansas cavalry for the Union army. (*Photos courtesy of the Arkansas History Commission*)

James H. Berry, as a young man

200

When the Civil War ended, many Confederates feared Union retribution and fled the country. A large number eventually settled in Mexico in the small village of Carlotta, seventy miles west of Vera Cruz. There, the Emperor had set aside the town and five hundred thousand acres of land for colonization by ex-Confederates. Thomas C. Hindman, a member of the colony, is shown here on October 22, 1865, with his three children, Susie, Tom, and Biscoe. Hindman tried farming and practicing law without much success. By late 1866, it was clear that ex-Confederates were not going to be treated badly by the Union authorities and in March, 1867, Hindman returned to his home in Helena, promising "to abide in good faith by the existing order of things."[9] However, Hindman's political radicalism and excesses while commanding in Arkansas had left behind a legacy of hatred toward him. On September 27, 1868, the general was sitting near an open window when he was mortally wounded by an assassin. One of the first men to arrive on the scene, James W. Hanks, wrote in his diary, "The scene was terrible[.] he had walked about after being shot and his blood was all over the place. It was a devilish horrible deed. No clue to the murderer yet."[10] And no clue was ever found. (*Photo courtesy of the Phillips County Museum, Helena, Arkansas*)

202

In the spring of 1861, Daniel Harris Reynolds, an attorney from Lake Village, Arkansas, raised a company of cavalry called the Chicot Rangers. The men elected young Reynolds captain, and they marched off to war. Reynolds went on to fight at Wilson's Creek, Pea Ridge, Chickamauga, Resaca, Atlanta, Franklin, and Nashville. Reynolds, now a brigadier general, had survived unharmed through some of the bloodiest battles in the west, but on March 19, 1865, at Bentonville, North Carolina, luck deserted him. There, in one of the last battles fought by the dwindling Confederate armies, a cannon ball mangled Reynolds' left leg. That evening, surgeons removed the leg just above the knee. Throughout the next month Reynolds suffered terribly. On April 20, he wrote: "I had a terrible spell with my wound this evening, the muscles commenced contracting & for more than an hour the pain was so intense that I was compelled to yield to 'cries of pain[.]' later in the night it got more quiet and I slept well."[11] On May 8, Reynolds had improved enough to walk on crutches and later that month he started the long journey home. On June 14, 1865, Reynolds reached Lake Village, and the next day he wrote in his diary, "the war is over & we failed."[12] During the coming months, hundreds of other amputees would also make their way back to Arkansas. (*Photo courtesy of Martha Ramseur Gillham*)

General Albert Pike was one of the prominent Arkansas Confederates who did not return to the state after the war. He had been military commander in the Department of the Indian Territory at the beginning of the war as well as Confederate Indian Commissioner. He had led his Indian troops into battle at Pea Ridge, but afterwards had run afoul of General Thomas Hindman and resigned his position. After the war he went to New York, then to Canada when he feared his possible arrest. He managed to receive a presidential pardon on August 30, 1865. He returned to the South in 1867 and settled in Memphis, Tennessee, where he edited the *Memphis Appeal* and may have been involved in the organization of the Ku Klux Klan. In 1868 he moved to Washington, D.C., where he worked as an attorney and as an associate editor of *The Patriot.* He was not, however, active in politics and spent most of his later years working on the ceremonies of the Free Masons. Pike died in Washington on April 2, 1891. (*Photo courtesy of the UALR Archives*)

Many Union soldiers saw political and financial opportunities in the defeated South and decided to remain behind after the war. Most of them soon became disenchanted and returned to their homes. However, some men such as Logan H. Roots remained and became prominent and wealthy citizens. Colonel Roots, who had earlier served with Generals Ulysses S. Grant and William T. Sherman, was ordered to Arkansas after the war had ended and mustered out in 1866.

Taking advantage of depressed land prices, Roots was soon successfully managing his newly acquired plantation near De Valls Bluff and dabbling in Republican politics. Between 1868 and 1871, Roots served in the U.S. Congress, but he lost his bid for a third term. Roots continued to be active in Republican political circles, but his real interests were shifting toward building his recently acquired Merchants' National Bank into one of the leading financial institutions in Arkansas. By the time of his death on March 30, 1893, Roots was recognized by his peers as the state's most prominent banker. Colonel Roots is shown seated in the middle with his quartermaster's staff that helped supply General Sherman's army on its famous 1864 March to the Sea. (*Photo courtesy of the UALR Archives*)

At the outbreak of the Civil War, twenty-five-year-old Joseph C. Barlow was working in Helena as a salesman in a local dry goods store. He immediately enlisted in the Phillips Guards then transferred to the Yell Rifles, and on June 30, 1862, he joined the Jackson Light Artillery. Barlow obtained the rank of captain and served with the battery in Tennessee, Mississippi, and Alabama. After the war ended he returned to Helena. Barlow went on to become a prominent businessman, but the war was never far from his memory.

On June 1, 1896, Barlow joined forty-three other local veterans to organize the Sam Corley Camp No. 841, of the United Confederate Veterans. The camp had been named in honor of Rev. Sam Corley, First Arkansas Cavalry, who was killed in 1863 at Fouche Bayou. The next year, members of No. 841 took a special train to the UCV's annual convention at Nashville, Tennessee. The round-trip ticket cost each veteran $6.70. During its history, at least 187 veterans were members of the camp, but by 1919, their ranks had been thinned to only 24 veterans. The last member of the camp, Captain C. L. Moore, Thirteenth Arkansas Infantry, died in 1931. This photo, which was probably taken in the early 1900s, shows seated from left to right: Captain Barlow, Major John J. Hornor—Thirteenth Arkansas, Adjutant J. T. Brame—First Virginia Regiment (Reserves). From left to right the standing members are: Captain C. N. Biscoe—Hindman's Legion, Captain E. W. Short—Twenty-fourth Alabama, and Private T. C. Ferguson—Thirteenth Arkansas Infantry. (*Photos courtesy of the Phillips County Library, Helena, Arkansas*)

In May, 1911, Confederate veterans began gathering in Little Rock for the 21st Annual Convention of the UCV. Throughout the city, hotels, friendly homes, makeshift sleeping quarters in schools, even tents—purchased with a Federal appropriation—were filling with more than twelve thousand old soldiers and thousands of sightseers. When the convention opened on May 16, Little Rock's population had swelled from 46,000 to 140,000 persons and the Reunion Committee had decorated over 100 city streets in patriotic attire. The finale of the convention came on May 18, when the Newton Bugle Corps signaled the beginning of the parade of old soldiers. After the leaders of the UCV and several bands passed in review, the Robert E. Lee Camp No. 1, in the place of honor, led the veterans down the parade route. In the Fourth, or Trans-Mississippi Division, men from Arkansas marched with their old comrades-in-arms. The next year, the UCV would meet in Macon, Georgia, but death would have further thinned their rapidly depleting ranks. (*Photo courtesy of the UALR Archives*)

The most influential Union veterans' organization was the Grand Army of the Republic, which began in 1866 and reached a peak strength in 1890 of 409,489 members. The GAR's Arkansas Department began in 1882, but by 1895 it contained only 1,006 members. The GAR, like the UCV, was organized in camps without regard to prior regimental affiliations. It served as both a social organization and a political lobbying arm for Union veterans. In addition to the GAR, many Union veterans continued to gather occasionally for regimental reunions. In this photo, the men of the Third Iowa Cavalry, which spent most of its time in Arkansas, are shown at their reunion. (*Photo courtesy of the Iowa State Historical Department*)

Throughout the South, one of the most popular and enduring methods for honoring the memory of the Confederacy was the construction of monuments. By the late nineteenth century, monument building had become almost an obsession, and in Arkansas, dozens of local groups were raising funds for particular projects. In Fort Smith, the Varina Davis Chapter of the United Daughters of the Confederacy, which had organized in 1898, decided that one of its first projects would be to raise funds for a suitable Confederate memorial for the city. Originally the UDC had planned to replace an older Confederate monument in the Na-

tional Cemetery which had been destroyed by a tornado, but Secretary of War Elihu Root refused to accept the UDC's plan for a statue of a Confederate soldier with the inscription "LEST WE FORGET." After showing much indignation about Mr. Root's effrontery, the UDC constructed the statue on the courthouse yard, where it stands today. In June 1903, Confederate veterans led by Brigadier General William L. Cabell (standing with a cane just to the left of the monument), attended the unveiling of the exact monument that Elihu Root had refused to approve. (*Photo courtesy of the Cravens Collection, UALR Archives*)

The above photographic collage was typical of the material produced after the war romanticizing and insuring the memory of the "Lost Cause." This particular *carte de visite* was made at Helena and includes several of the prominent Confederate figures from Arkansas as well as those from elsewhere in the South. Included are Albert Pike, William Hardee, Thomas Hindman, Sterling Price, and Patrick Cleburne. (*Photo courtesy of the Phillips County Museum*)

The influence of ex-Confederates and their political allies became apparent on April 1, 1891, when Governor James P. Eagle signed into law legislation of far-reaching consequences for Arkansans who had served the Confederacy. The act provided pensions for certain disabled veterans or their widows, and it also appropriated funds to build a home for needy ex-soldiers. The home, which opened its doors in 1892, originally housed only males, but in the early twentieth century, the General Assembly appropriated funds to construct an annex for widows. As late as 1920, 165 persons were still living in the home. Nearby was the old Confederate burial ground, which later became part of the National Cemetery. For many years, the local UDC chapter cared for these Confederate graves, and helped raise money to pay for the burial of other veterans. (*Photo courtesy of the J. N. Heiskell Historical Collection, UALR Archives*)

By the 1920's, death had greatly reduced the number of Civil War veterans, but those who remained still liked to reminisce about their adventures. The old soldier on the left—Benjamin C. Martin, who had served with the Union in Company B, Fifteenth Missouri Cavalry, is chatting with Confederate veteran J. Wade Sikes who fought with the Second Arkansas Mounted Infantry at Pea Ridge. During the War, Sikes also turned to preaching. He stayed with the Second Arkansas until the summer of 1864 when he lost his left arm in the Atlanta campaign. After the war, Sikes returned to northwest Arkansas where he practiced law and was elected the first mayor of Rogers. At the age of 92, he was still active enough to travel to Little Rock to argue a case before the Supreme Court. Sikes, an avid fox hunter, once said that the most beautiful sounds in the world to him were the rebel yell and the deep baying of hounds on the chase. Martin died in 1946. Sikes died in 1929. This photo was taken in Rogers probably in the mid 1920s. Perhaps they are discussing the war. (*Photo courtesy of the J. N. Heiskell Historical Collection, UALR Archives*)

Appendix

Bailey, R. Jesse

Bailey, a Virginian, enlisted in the 3d Arkansas Infantry on March 17, 1862. He surrendered at Appomattox on April 9, 1865. He apparently remained in Virginia after the war, although he moved to Arkansas in 1888. In June, 1917, he applied for a pension, which he received on the grounds that he was partially blind, suffered from nerve related disease, and had a left wrist that had never healed from an earlier fracture. The state of Arkansas awarded him a pension of one hundred dollars. In 1923 he moved into the Arkansas Confederate Home, but remained only a year. After that time he left, and simply disappeared. Bailey never married.

Baird, John M. W.

Baird continued service with the 1st Arkansas throughout the war. He was captured by Federal cavalry at Macon, Georgia, in April, 1865, and was released at the end of the war. He did not return to Jackson County after the war.

Barlow, Joseph Cantrell

Barlow served in the artillery through the war and surrendered as a part of General Richard Taylor's Department of Alabama, Mississippi, and East Louisiana on May 11, 1865. After the war he moved to Memphis where he worked as a clerk for a year, then returned to Helena. Barlow spent the rest of his life in that town where he owned a hardware store. He was active in politics. He commanded a cavalry force of citizens hostile to local Republican government during the Reconstruction. Barlow also served several terms as mayor of Helena. In 1882 he was appointed to head the Arkansas State Guards. He died on September 17, 1920, in Helena at the age of eighty-five.

Baxter, Elisha

After leaving the governor's office in 1874, Baxter tried unsuccessfully in 1878 to gain a seat from Arkansas in the United States Senate. After that election he withdrew from politics and lived on a small farm near Batesville until his death in 1899.

Becton, Jacob G.

Becton was born in North Carolina, October 23, 1833, and moved to Arkansas in March, 1861. His first home was Prairie County. In February, 1862, he enlisted in Captain Bull's company, 17th Arkansas Mounted Infantry, Lemoine's Brigade. This later became part of the 21st Arkansas Mounted Infantry which was captured at the Battle of Champion Hill. Becton was sent to a Federal prison at Johnson's Island, Ohio, and later exchanged. He reentered the service and was captured again on May 3, 1865, at De Valls Bluff by the 9th Kansas Cavalry. After the war he farmed 960 acres of land near Des Arc, and he owned a cotton gin. He was prominent in his community, a member of the Masonic Lodge and the Methodist Episcopal Church South. He died of pneumonia on February 26, 1906.

Behen, Denis

Behen served with the 37th Arkansas Infantry through the rest of the war and apparently mustered out with it sometime in the spring of 1865.

Berry, James Henderson

When Senator Augustus H. Garland resigned his Senate seat to become attorney general under President Grover Cleveland, the state legislature elected Berry to fill the unexpired term. Berry took office on March 25, 1885, and remained there for the next twenty-two years. In 1906, Berry lost his seat to Jeff Davis and retired to his home in Bentonville. He was the last Confederate veteran to represent Arkansas in the United States Senate. During retirement, Berry maintained his long interest in the United Confederate Veterans. In 1910, the secretary of war appointed him commissioner to mark the graves of Confederate soldiers who died in

Union prisons. Berry completed his work in December, 1912, and died the following January, 1913.

Blake, John T.

After the war, Blake returned to Kansas City, Missouri, and married Annie L. Maxwell in 1866. For many years he contracted with the Federal government to deliver quartermaster supplies to army outposts in the west and to carry the overland mails. Except for a brief period between 1878 and 1886, when Blake lived in Colorado, his home was in Missouri. Blake's business interests, however, necessarily meant that he traveled frequently on the western frontier. Blake was an active member of the Republican Party after the war and was on the state central committees in Colorado and Missouri. He died of tuberculosis on April 13, 1899, in his home in Kansas City.

Blunt, James G.

Blunt continued to serve in the Trans-Mississippi West throughout the war, but his outspoken criticism of his superiors and his habit of sharing his views with President Lincoln eventually caused his downfall. In October, 1863, he was removed from his command of the District of the Frontier and reassigned to an obscure post in Kansas. After the war, Blunt remained in Kansas for four years practicing medicine. He later moved to Washington, D.C., where he worked for many years as a claims agent. He spent his last few years in a government hospital for the insane, where he died on July 27, 1881.

Bogy, Joseph Vital

After being paroled following his capture at Vicksburg, Bogy reenlisted in the 2nd Missouri Battery. He served with this unit under Johnston and Hood in Georgia. At the end of the war he was at Gainesville, Alabama, where Bogy surrendered on May 4, 1865. Bogy married Ruth

Smith, a woman he had met in Alabama during the war. They returned to Pine Bluff, where they lived until 1874. In that year they moved to Texas where Bogy farmed at Willow Point. For nine years he was the postmaster at Willow Point. J. V. Bogy died on July 25, 1914; his wife died on March 26, 1926.

Boon, Jacob

Private Boon did not survive the war. The photograph was taken in Keokuk, Iowa, several months before his death. Boon was probably returning to Arkansas from leave when he was accidentally killed on December 17, 1864, in an explosion aboard the steamer *Maria.*

Bragg, Junius

Bragg returned to Camden after the war and practiced medicine. He died on October 2, 1900, in St. Vincent's Institute, St. Louis, Missouri, where he was being treated for an illness.

Buford, Napoleon Bonaparte

Buford mustered out of the United States Army in August, 1865, and briefly held several successive Federal appointments. He later moved to Chicago, where he died on March 28, 1883.

Cabell, William Lewis

Cabell resided in Fort Smith after the war. He studied law and was admitted to the bar there. In 1872, he moved to Dallas, Texas, where he served four terms as mayor. For many years, Cabell was commander of the Trans-Mississippi Department of the United Confederate Veterans. He died in Dallas on February 22, 1911.

Clements, Henry

Clements served with the 1st Arkansas throughout the war. He was captured near Jonesboro, Georgia, on September 1, 1864, but exchanged almost immediately. He surrendered with his unit at Milledgeville, Georgia, on May 4, 1865,

and took the oath of amnesty eight days later. Clements did not return to Jackson County.

Cloud, William F.

After the battle at Prairie Grove, Colonel Cloud and the 2d Kansas Cavalry spent much of their time patrolling northwest Arkansas, southwest Missouri, and the Indian Territory. When the war ended Cloud and his men were transferred to Fort Gibson, Cherokee Nation, where they remained on duty until July 2, 1865. The 2d Kansas mustered out of the service on August 17, 1865, but Cloud was recommissioned as a colonel in the 15th Kansas and operated against the Indians. In 1867, he moved to Carthage, Missouri, where he practiced law and sold real estate. Cloud became active in Republican politics. He served for many years as county committeeman and was elected as a representative in the Twenty-sixth Missouri General Assembly. In 1876, Cloud was appointed collector of internal revenue, a position that he apparently held until 1882, when he was an unsuccessful candidate for the U.S. Congress. Sometime in the mid-1890s, Cloud moved to Kansas City, Missouri, where he wrote several books on topics as diverse as Mexican politics and the Boer War. He died at his home on March 4, 1905.

Coombs, George

Coombs remained with the battery through the rest of the war. He returned with it to Iowa in the fall of 1865, mustering out at Davenport on October 23.

Cross, David C.

In December, 1861, Colonel Cross contracted pneumonia, and on May 12, 1862, left the 5th Arkansas at Corinth. He returned to his land holdings in Poinsett County. Still in ill health, Cross worked for the creation of Cross County and allowed the new county government to meet in his home. After the war he moved to Memphis, although maintaining extensive plantation interests in Arkansas. He was an incorporator of the Crittenden and Cross County Leveed Road Company and the Iron Mountain and Helena Railroad. In 1871 he became president of the latter and the following year sold 40,000 acres of his land to keep that line out of bankruptcy. He was never in good health after the war, and on August 21, 1874, he died at the home of his friend Willis Perry Wilkins, and was buried in the Wilkins family cemetery. His gravestone reads:

In loving memory of Col. D. C. Cross, who raised the 5th Ark. Inf. Reg. in April 1861, and for whom Cross County is Named. Born in Gates County, N.C. in 1818. Died August 21, 1874.

Crump, William Wallace

Crump continued to serve in the Confederate army until sometime in January or February of 1864 when he was left by his unit at Pine Bluff because he was suffering from some illness. He recovered enough to go home, but was never fully well afterwards. He and his wife moved to Oklahoma sometime after the war where he remained until his death. His wife then returned to Arkansas.

Curtis, Samuel Ryan

After Curtis left Helena, he held various commands in Missouri, Kansas, and the Northwest. In August, 1865, he was commissioned to negotiate several treaties with the Indian tribes of the Great Plains. Curtis then went to work for the Union Pacific Railroad which was constructing rails in western Iowa. He died at Council Bluffs, Iowa, on December 26, 1866.

DeWolf, Charles

The 7th Missouri went on to campaign with General Steele in the Little Rock and Camden expeditions. DeWolf remained with his regiment until March 4, 1864, when he was medically discharged because his sight was almost gone. DeWolf finally settled in Garnett, Kansas, where he became a successful businessman. Throughout his life DeWolf remained interested in the battle of Prairie Grove, and in 1906, he helped organize a reunion of old soldiers who had fought there. He died on March 23, 1927, at the age of ninety-three.

Dobbins, Archibald

When the war ended, Dobbins fled the country and drifted southward into Latin America. On June 5, 1867, he wrote his wife that he was in Brazil and that "I never intend to return to the States on account of my political difficulties." Dobbins originally began farming at Santarem near the junction of the Tapajos and Amazon rivers. By August, 1869, he had moved farther into the jungle to the village of Itartuba, where he lived with "Indians and mixed bloods."* Shortly afterwards the letters to his wife ended, and Dobbins was never heard from again.

Elliott, George

Elliott died of pneumonia at Camp Douglas, Chicago, Illinois, on May 3, 1862.

Fagan, James

Major General James Fagan commanded the District of Arkansas in the waning days of the Confederacy. After the war, he returned to Little Rock, where he eventually began an insurance company. In 1872, Fagan joined the Republican insurgents led by Joseph Brooks, who were trying to overthrow Powell Clayton's hand-picked successor, Elisha Baxter. Fagan commanded Brooks' militia in the short-lived Brooks-Baxter war that had erupted over the disputed gubernatorial election. Fagan's identification with the Republicans discredited him with many ex-Confederates, as did his later appointments as a U.S. marshal and receiver of government lands. Fagan died in Little Rock on September 1, 1893.

*Bob Dolehite, "Arch S. Dobbins," *Phillips County Historical Quarterly* IV (September, 1965): 21–23.

Fletcher, John Gould, Sr.

Fletcher returned to Little Rock on April 26, 1865. He went into the general merchandise business with a fellow member of the Capitol Guards, Peter Hotze. This business rapidly expanded to include the buying and selling of cotton, with the opening of a branch in New York City in 1873. Fletcher remained in Little Rock while Hotze moved to New York. The firm became one of the leading cotton exchanges in the South and continued until 1902 when the two retired. In 1874, Fletcher was an unsuccessful candidate for the Constitutional Convention. He was mayor of Little Rock from 1875 until 1881 and was elected Pulaski County Sheriff in 1884. Nominated for governor three times, the last time in 1900, he represented the conservative wing of the Democratic Party against Jeff Davis. He was concerned with veterans affairs and was one of the founders of the Confederate rest home at Sweet Home. He was married to Pauline Kraus in 1877. He died January 31, 1907, and was buried at Mount Holly Cemetery in Little Rock.

Gillet, Orville

Gillet remained in Arkansas for a time after mustering out of the service. On June 29, 1865, he married Julia Ann Dacus, sister of Robert H. Dacus of the 1st Arkansas Mounted Rifles (Confederate). The couple moved to Reese, Michigan, where they lived until 1907 when they moved to Little Rock. Gillet died at Little Rock on October 30, 1914, and is buried at the Little Rock National Cemetery.

Granger, William W.

Granger was discharged from the army on March 13, 1864, because of failing sight in his left eye. His wife joined him in Little Rock, where Granger practiced medicine until about 1872. He moved that year to Washington, D.C., where he worked in the District's engineering department until his vision was almost com-

pletely gone. Granger spent the last years of his life totally disabled. He died at Fairmont, West Virginia, on November 30, 1898.

Gratiot, John R.

After the Battle of Wilson's Creek, Gratiot returned to Washington, Arkansas, and became the county surveyor, a post that he had held before the war. Gratiot served as surveyor from 1862 until 1866, then again from 1872 to 1880. He died at Washington on April 14, 1891.

Greaves, Peter B.

Greaves survived the war and remained with his regiment until it was mustered out at Austin, Texas, on February 15, 1866. He apparently returned with it to Davenport, Iowa.

Grinsted, Hiram L.

Colonel Grinsted died on April 30, 1864, while leading his regiment at the Battle of Jenkins' Ferry. He was buried in Camden, Arkansas.

Halliburton, William A.

Halliburton was captured near Jonesboro, Georgia, on September 1, 1864. After being exchanged at Rough and Ready, Georgia, he returned to his home in Stone County. On December 23, 1866, he married Mary Parlee Conditt and the two had seven children. In 1879, he purchased 40 acres of land that he farmed. By the time of his death his operations embraced over 600 acres of land. He was a member of the Missionary Baptist Church. Halliburton's wife died in 1922 and he died in 1927. Both are buried in Evetts Cemetery in Stone County.

Hardee, William J.

Hardee left Arkansas and joined the Confederate forces in Kentucky. He fought later at Shiloh, Murfreesboro, Chattanooga, and Atlanta. He surrendered in North Carolina in April, 1865. After the war, he settled in Selma, Alabama, where he became a planter. Hardee died on November 6, 1873, while traveling through Virginia.

Harvey, Aaron

Harvey had been a slave in South Carolina for most of his life before the war. In 1858, however, he had been sold and moved to Mississippi. When Union forces occupied Helena, Harvey assisted others in using a plan to swim the Mississippi River to seek freedom. He joined the Union forces at Helena. After the war he continued in the service until he was honorably discharged at Leavenworth, Kansas on December 13, 1866. He moved to Little Rock and was married. He died at Little Rock on April 8, 1934.

Herron, Francis J.

Shortly after Prairie Grove, Herron was appointed major general to rank from November 29, 1862. He was the youngest major general to fight for either side. He later served at Vicksburg and commanded the XIIIth Corps at Brownsville, Texas. During Reconstruction he was a U.S. marshal, and later acted as secretary of state in Louisiana. In 1877, Herron moved to New York where he died on January 8, 1902, in a tenement on West 99th Street. At the time, Herron was unemployed.

Hill, Henry A.

Hill was apparently killed in the trench warfare around Atlanta in late July, 1864.

Hindman, Thomas C.

Hindman returned to Helena after the war where he became involved in Conservative and Democratic politics. He was assassinated at his home on September 27, 1868.

Holcomb, William Henry

Holcomb enlisted in Company G, 15th Arkansas Infantry on November 1, 1861, at Camp McCulloch. In June, 1862, he was appointed

captain. He received wounds at Corinth and also at Pea Ridge. He was captured at Big Black Bridge on May 17, 1863, and went to Johnson's Island where he remained until the end of the war. Then he returned to Washington County and became a farmer and merchant near Springdale. In 1879 he owned 207 acres in the county. He died at Springdale on July 11, 1890.

Holmes, Theophilus Hunter

Holmes eventually was relieved of command in the Trans-Mississippi West and returned to North Carolina where he helped organize home guard units. After the war he returned to his small farm in Cumberland County, North Carolina, and died there on June 21, 1880.

Johnson, Robert W.

United States Senator Robert W. Johnson was sent by the Arkansas legislature as a delegate to the Confederate Congress following secession. The state legislature later elected him to serve in the Confederate Senate. In Richmond, Johnson pushed for the allocation of men and resources to Arkansas and was a thorn in the side of President Jefferson Davis. After the war he considered fleeing to Mexico, but decided to return to Arkansas. He dabbled in politics for a time, but failed to recapture his position or to regain his fortune. He ran for the Senate again in 1878, but lost to James D. Walker, son of Judge David Walker. He finally moved to Washington, D.C., where he practiced law with Albert Pike. He died in Little Rock on July 26, 1879, and is buried in Mount Holly Cemetery.

Keyes, Clark

Keyes, who could neither read nor write, returned to Michigan after the war, and apparently spent much of his life as a laborer. His first wife died on July 13, 1896, and shortly afterward, Keyes moved into the Michigan Soldiers' Home in Kent County. He was nearly blind and had no money other than his monthly veteran's pension of twelve dollars. On October 10, 1899, Keyes married Maria Smith and the couple moved to Milford, Michigan, where he died on September 12, 1911. Sometime after his death, Maria moved to the Michigan Soldiers' Home, where she died on July 7, 1923.

Lee, P. Lynch

This cousin of Robert E. Lee was captured with his unit at Fort Henry and imprisoned at Fort Warren until the autumn of 1862. He returned to Arkansas, rejoined his unit, and was captured at Port Hudson, where he was also wounded. He was sent to Johnson's Island and remained in Federal prison camps until May, 1865. He returned to his home in Camden, where he clerked on a steamboat that operated between that town and New Orleans. In 1872 he was elected the first post-war Democratic sheriff of Ouachita County. He was active in many local organizations. He was a member of the Episcopal Church. He died at Camden on May 9, 1911.

Lyon, Nathaniel

Lyon was killed on August 10, 1861, at Wilson's Creek.

Lyon, Orlo Henry

Following the war, Lyon returned to Rockford, Iowa, where he had taught school before the war. He married Belle A. Bradford in 1867, and the couple had seven children. Between 1871 and 1877 Lyon was postmaster at Rockford. In 1877 he became editor of the Rockford *Reveille* and also entered banking. He served one term in the state legislature. In 1883 Lyon became president of the First National Bank at Rockford and he held that position until he retired in 1903. Lyon died on June 18, 1903.

Main, William H.

Sergeant Main mustered out of the army on October 23, 1865, and later married Sophie Boddingen in Independence, Iowa, on November 2, 1869. Main and his wife eventually settled in

San Francisco where he worked as a laborer in the United States Mint. On March 23, 1901, Main was granted a medical pension of six dollars per month because of "partial inability to earn a support by manual labor." He died on January 8, 1906, and is buried in the San Francisco National Cemetery, grave number 319.

Manning, Hartrog Vanney "Vann"

When Federal authorities finally released Manning from prison, he moved to Holly Springs, Mississippi. Manning practiced law there until 1877, when he was elected to the United States Congress. He remained in Congress until 1883, when fellow members ruled against his election in a disputed race. Manning remained in Washington, D.C., and practiced law there until his death on November 3, 1892.

Marmaduke, John S.

After the fall of Little Rock, Marmaduke withdrew to the South with the retreating Confederates. He continued to serve in the Trans-Mississippi and accompanied Sterling Price on his raid into Missouri. On October 25, 1864, Marmaduke was captured at Mine Creek, Kansas. While in prison, he was appointed a major general of the Confederate army. After the war, he returned to Missouri where he engaged in business and edited an agricultural journal. In 1884, he was elected governor, but died on December 28, 1887, shortly before the expiration of his term.

Martin, Benjamin

Martin mustered out of the 15th Missouri in 1865 and returned home to Missouri. In 1878 he moved to Benton County, Arkansas, where he farmed near Rogers. He died on October 28, 1946, at the age of 101, the oldest Union army veteran in Benton County.

Mathews, Robert P.

Surgeons were unable to remove the rifle ball that had penetrated Mathews' right lung, and he was discharged from service. Mathews returned to his home in Greene County, Missouri, where he farmed and occasionally taught school. In 1870 he was elected county judge, a position that he held for four years. Throughout his life the wound he received at Pea Ridge caused recurring pulmonary problems. Finally in the winter of 1891 he contracted pneumonia and died on December 19. At the time of his death, Mathews was working as the deputy recorder of deeds for Greene County. He left behind a wife and eight children. Mathews was actively involved in the agrarian, labor, and religious reform movements that occurred in the late nineteenth century. Shortly before his death, his friend and fellow ex-soldier Colonel Sempronius H. Boyd described Mathews as an independent thinking man who had had the "distinguished honor of being a religious and political mugwump."

May, George E.

May enrolled in the 2d Arkansas Mounted Rifles at Camp McRae on July 26, 1861. In October, he was on sick leave, but returned to his unit in January, 1862. In March, 1862, he was assigned to the Confederate hospital at Little Rock as a nurse. He deserted on January 8, 1864.

May, James M.

May surrendered with the 23d Arkansas Infantry at Marshall, Texas, in 1865. He returned to his family farm in Clark County. He became a prosperous farmer, and constructed one of the first steam gins in the county. He died at Okolona from Bright's Disease in November, 1912.

McCollum, John N.

Following his resignation in 1862, McCollum returned to Arkansas. Rather than staying at home, he enlisted on the Union side, joining the 4th Arkansas Cavalry at Little Rock in December, 1863. He apparently remained in Arkansas after the war, applying for a pension in 1897.

McCown, Simon

After Wilson's Creek, McCown, along with almost all the Arkansas state troops, resigned from the army. He later reenlisted in Co. I, 19th Arkansas Infantry and fought at Pea Ridge. On January 11, 1863, most of the 19th surrendered at Arkansas Post, but Company I managed to escape. McCown's unit served in Arkansas for the remainder of the war. When the war ended, McCown returned to his farm near Nashville. He died at his home on March 8, 1892.

McCulloch, Benjamin

McCulloch died at Pea Ridge on March 7, 1862.

McCulloch, Clem

McCulloch returned to Fort Smith when the Arkansas troops disbanded after the Battle of Wilson's Creek. He worked there as a clerk until July 20, 1862, when he joined Company B, 34th Arkansas Infantry. He went on to fight at Helena, Prairie Grove, and Jenkins' Ferry. After the war he entered Cane Hill College, and married Amanda Campbell Lacy. McCulloch worked in the state auditor's office for many years and spent much of his time writing about his Civil War experiences. He died in Little Rock on May 5, 1911.

McCulloch, Robert

McCulloch and his command were transferred to Mississippi with Van Dorn's army. He later served with General Nathan B. Forrest's cavalry and was severely wounded twice. McCulloch surrendered with Lieutenant General Richard Taylor's troops on May 4, 1865. Only 191 men of the original complement of 871 cavalrymen were still present for duty. He returned to his farm in Cooper County, Missouri, and entered local politics. From 1872 to 1876, McCulloch was collector, and in 1878, he was elected sheriff. In 1880, he was elected registrar of state lands, and was reelected until 1892. In 1895, he was selected as the local commander of Camp 417 of the United Confederate Veterans.

McCullum, Hugh

McCullum was killed at Jenkins' Ferry on April 30, 1864.

McIntosh, James M.

McIntosh was killed at Pea Ridge on March 7, 1862, during a cavalry charge at the battle of Pea Ridge. His body was carried to Fort Smith, where he is now buried in the National Cemetery.

Messick, Elisha H.

Messick was captured at Port Hudson. Because he was an officer he was not returned but sent to a Northern prison. He apparently remained a prisoner until the end of the war. After his release he did not return to Arkansas.

Miller, Edward G.

The 20th Wisconsin saw no more action in Arkansas. After mustering out of the service on August 8, 1865, Miller returned to Wisconsin and married. He later moved to Iowa, and began farming. In 1873, he was elected to the state senate. Miller served two terms and sponsored the bill that created the Iowa State Teacher's College. Like many veterans, he became active in the Grand Army of the Republic, and briefly served as a department commander. In 1877, Miller went to work as a railway postal clerk, a position he held until his death on Memorial Day, 1906.

Moore, George W.

Moore survived the war and was mustered out of the army at Memphis, Tennessee, on August 20, 1865. He apparently did not remain in Arkansas.

Morton, William F.

Morton survived the war and remained in Mississippi.

Murphy, Isaac

After the secession convention, Murphy returned to Madison County and attempted to resume life as a schoolmaster. Eventually, partisan pressure forced him to flee to Union lines for protection. On March 6, 1864, Murphy was elected governor under Abraham Lincoln's reconstruction plan. As a wartime governor, Murphy faced enormous problems, and even though he accomplished little during his administration, he did act with magnanimity toward former Confederates. However, his pleas for moderation were swept aside during Congressional Reconstruction, and Murphy did not run for a second term. He returned to Madison County where he farmed and practiced law until his death on September 8, 1882.

Noble, Mark

Mark Noble served during the entire war in the 2d Arkansas Cavalry, rising from corporal to lieutenant in the three years of his service. He was captured at the end of the war in Jefferson County on May 6, 1865, and confined to the military prison at Little Rock until finally released on June 10, 1865. He returned to his family and spent the rest of his life farming near Crossett in Ashley County. He was a Mason. In 1912 he received a state pension. His application indicated that he was in a generally senile condition and suffering from heart trouble, the result of advanced age. His wife Sarah died on April 22, 1919, and he died on June 16, 1919, and both were buried at Bethel Cemetery near their home.

Oates, Calvin Grier

Private Oates was moved to a prisoner-of-war camp at Alton, Illinois. He was eventually exchanged for Jerry Phelan, an Arkansas Union-ist, and rejoined his company at Priceville, Mis-sissippi. Oates then fought at Murfreesboro, where he was wounded in the chest. On July 17, 1863, Private Oates deserted and went to Texas. When the war ended, he returned to his home in Pottsville and resumed farming. In his later years, Oates often acted as a witness for Con-federate veterans who were applying for pen-sions. He died in 1914 at the age of 71, and was buried at the Pisgha cemetery.

Osterhaus, Peter J.

After the Battle of Pea Ridge, Osterhaus was appointed brigadier general. He went on to be-come one of the Union's most distinguished foreign-born officers, fighting at Vicksburg, Missionary Ridge, the Atlanta campaign, and in Sherman's march through Georgia and the Carolinas. After the war, he served as United States Consul in both France and Germany. At the age of ninety-four, he died on January 2, 1917, in Coblenz, Germany, just three months before the United States entered World War I.

Patton, Andrew

Patton was with the 60th U.S. Colored when it mustered out of service at De Valls Bluff on Oc-tober 15, 1865. He eventually settled in Mis-souri where he died in the early 1890s.

Phelps, John E.

The 2d Arkansas Cavalry (Union) operated in Arkansas and Missouri until January, 1865, when the regiment was transferred to Memphis, Tennessee. Phelps was then a brevet brigadier general. He suffered severely by the end of the war from medical problems that resulted from malaria that he had contracted at Vicksburg. His doctor recommended that his military service continue, although outside a southern climate. Instead, he was mustered out of the army at Memphis, Tennessee, on August 20, 1865, and returned to his home in Greene County, Mis-souri. In 1867, Phelps was appointed receiver of public money, but was later removed by Presi-dent Ulysses S. Grant because he was a Demo-crat. During the 1880s Phelps, at various times, engaged in the mercantile business, farming, zinc mining, and mail contracting. Like many ex-soldiers, Phelps was active in the Grand Army of the Republic and served a number of years as Grand Commander of the Missouri Department in that organization. Sometime after 1893 Phelps moved to Washington state and then to California, where he died Septem-ber 17, 1921, at Pasadena.

Pike, Albert

Pike became an attorney in Washington, D.C., after the war, and he died there on April 2, 1891.

Porter, Stephen K.

Porter died on December 18, 1862, after con-tracting fever at Cotton Plant, Arkansas.

Pratt, Theodore

Pratt was killed at Big Creek on July 25, 1864.

Price, Sterling

Price remained in the Confederate army through-out the war. When the conflict ended, he, like many other high-ranking officials, feared that the victorious Union would punish him, and he fled to Mexico. In 1866, Price returned to Mis-souri where he died the following year.

Ramsaur, Lee M.

Ramsaur returned to his unit after Wilson's Creek and fought until he was badly wounded at Murfreesboro, Tennessee. The wound dis-abled him for further service. After the war, he returned to his law practice in Augusta, Wood-ruff County. He was elected to the Arkansas General Assembly in 1866 and served only one term. Ramsaur briefly held public office again as county judge in Woodruff County between

1874 and 1876. He practiced law until his death on August 14, 1881.

Rayburn, Doc

Rayburn was rumored to have been killed by one of his own men shortly after the war ended, but this has never been confirmed. Tradition maintains that he was buried in an unmarked grave near Des Arc.

Rector, Henry Massie

As Arkansas' first Confederate governor, Rector presided over the mobilization of the state and remained in office throughout most of the disastrous months of 1862. On October 6, 1862, Rector was defeated for reelection by Harris Flanagin. He later served as a private in the state reserve corps. Two of his sons died in the Confederate armies. In 1865, Rector again resumed management of his plantations in Hempstead, Garland, and Pulaski counties. He died in Little Rock on August 12, 1899, and is buried in Mount Holly Cemetery.

Reynolds, Daniel Harris

Reynolds returned to his home in Lake Village after the war ended. From 1866 to 1867, he served in the state senate. Afterwards he practiced law in his home town until his death on March 14, 1902.

Rice, Samuel R.

Rice was sent to his home in Oskalooga, Iowa, to recuperate from the wound he received at Jenkins' Ferry. However, the injury became infected, and he died on July 6, 1864.

Richardson, Sam J.

Richardson and many other officers captured at Arkansas Post were imprisoned at Camp Chase, Ohio. In May, 1863, he was exchanged in Virginia and returned to the Trans-Mississippi theater. Between December, 1863, and July, 1864,

he and his unit guarded Federal prisoners at Tyler, Texas, and hunted for Confederate deserters in the surrounding counties. In the summer of 1864, the unit joined General E. Kirby Smith's forces in Louisiana and surrendered with them on May 26, 1865. He returned to his farm near Marshall in Harrison County, Texas. In 1866, he was elected to the House of Representatives in the state legislature. In 1867, he was chief of police at Marshall where he demonstrated great hostility to Reconstruction efforts, personally breaking up one political rally and causing what became known as the "Marshall Riot." He was arrested by military authorities but released. He continued to be active in politics, serving on the country's "conservative" central committee in 1867 and 1868.

Roots, Logan H.

Roots retired from banking in 1890 because of ill health. He died on March 30, 1893, at Little Rock.

Ryan, Abraham H.

Colonel Ryan mustered out of the army on June 30, 1865, and possibly returned to his home in Peoria, Illinois. On March 26, 1879, he married Emma A. Harris at Monticello, New York, and in 1880, they settled in East Orange, New Jersey. Ryan, a businessman, became the first president of Savers Investment and Trust Co., and later became the director of the People's Bank at East Orange. Ryan died suddenly on December 2, 1903. He was aboard a Lackawanna train en route from New York City to his home.

Sala, Orlando P.

Private Sala mustered out of the 1st Iowa Cavalry in Austin, Texas, on February 15, 1866. He returned to Iowa and entered medical school, and began practice in 1869. Throughout most of the remainder of his life, Sala lived in Bloomington, Wisconsin. His first wife, Mary, died on November 14, 1880, and his second wife, Alice, died on December 16, 1896. On May 21, 1897, Sala married Ella Bohringer, and they lived together until Sala's death on April 24, 1914.

Scott, Christopher T.

After the war, Scott returned to Camden where he entered the mercantile business. In 1869 he moved to Arkadelphia and founded the firm of Scott and Company. By 1870 he had joined Smoker Mercantile, and he remained there until about 1895. In the 1870s he helped found the first Episcopal church in Arkadelphia, St. Michael's. When the congregation dwindled, Scott became a Methodist. For years he was a member of the Board of the Arkadelphia School District. He died on June 26, 1920, and was buried at Rose Hill Cemetery in Arkadelphia.

Sebastian, William K.

Senator Sebastian died in Memphis, Tennessee, on May 20, 1865.

Shelby, Orville Joseph

When the war ended, Shelby and a few of his cavalrymen buried their battle flags in the Rio Grande River, and fled to Mexico. After the fall of Emperor Maximilian's empire, Shelby returned to his home in Missouri. In 1893, President Grover Cleveland appointed him United States Marshal of the Western District of Missouri, a position that he held until his death in Adrian, Missouri, on February 18, 1897.

Shores, William

Shores was wounded at Murfreesboro, and died on January 7, 1863.

Sigel, Franz

Shortly after Pea Ridge, Sigel was transferred to the eastern theater of operations, where his military shortcomings became obvious. While serving there, he had the misfortune to be trounced soundly at New Market, Virginia, on May 15, 1864, by a hastily improvised force which included a battalion of cadets from the Virginia Military Institute. After the war, Sigel remained active in politics until his death in New York City on August 21, 1902.

Sikes, J. Wade

Sikes died in Rogers, Arkansas, on January 7, 1929, at the age of 101.

Slemons, William Ferguson

Slemons returned to his home in Monticello after the war and resumed the practice of law. Between 1866 and 1868, Slemons served as prosecuting attorney. He was later elected to Congress and served three terms between 1875 and 1881. Slemons declined to run for a fourth term and resumed his law practice. From 1903 to 1907 he served as county judge in Drew County. In 1908, he was elected Justice of the Peace, and held that position until his death on December 10, 1918. He is buried in Union Hill Cemetery near Monticello.

Squires, Charles

Private Squires was discharged from the service on September 29, 1864, and two months later he married Barbara H. Cathcart. The couple moved to Nebraska where they lived and probably farmed until the late 1880s. The Squires then moved to South Dakota for a few years, and eventually settled in Olympia, Washington. Squires died on December 5, 1909. After his death, 66-year-old Barbara applied for her widow's pension, stating that she "was without means of support other than her daily labor."

Stark, Charles S.

Captain Stark organized Company B, 1st Arkansas Infantry in May of 1861. In July, 1862, Stark resigned his commission and left Confederate service in Arkansas. He survived the war and moved to Georgia. He died at Athens, Georgia, on October 4, 1899.

Steele, Frederick

Steele relinquished command of the Department of Arkansas on December 27, 1864, and assumed control of the District of West Florida. After the war, Steele, a professional soldier, was appointed colonel of the 20th United States Infantry, and later served as the commander of the Department of Columbia. Steele was killed in a buggy accident at San Mateo, California, on January 12, 1868.

Stillwell, Leander

Stillwell, who served in Company D, 61st Illinois Infantry, recovered from his illness and was with his unit until the end of the war. Stillwell studied law at Albany, New York, after the war, and was admitted to the bar in December, 1867. In 1868 he began his practice in Erie, Kansas. In 1877, Stillwell was elected to the Kansas House of Representatives where he served one term. In 1883, he was elected judge of the 7th Judicial District and remained in office until September, 1907, when he resigned because his wife was dying. On November 25, 1909, President William H. Taft appointed Judge Stillwell as first deputy commissioner of pensions. Stillwell moved to Washington where he apparently remained until Taft left office in 1913. He then returned to his home in Kansas, where he died in 1934. During his life, Stillwell occasionally wrote about his experiences in the Civil War. One of his works, "Scenes at Shiloh," won first place in the 1890 *New York Tribune* competition for Civil War reminiscences, but Stillwell's best known work was his autobiography, *The Story of a Common Soldier,* which was published in 1917.

Tappan, James C.

General Tappan later fought at Jenkins' Ferry and Pleasant Hill, Louisiana, and took part in Price's 1864 Missouri raid. After the war, he resumed his law practice in Helena, and served two terms in the Arkansas General Assembly. He died on March 19, 1906.

Thomas, John J.

Imprisoned in the North during the last two years of the war, Thomas returned to Washington in Hempstead County afterwards and married Sarah Holt, daughter of County Judge Milton Holt. They had two children. He practiced farming and also went into the lumber business. In 1869 he constructed an architecturally noteworthy one-story frame house northeast of Washington with lumber provided by his father-in-law. He was on the State Board of Charities. He also was a representative of the Lesser Goldman Cotton Company of St. Louis in Hempstead County. He lived outside of Washington until his death on December 21, 1920.

Thompson, Meriwether Jeff

After Thompson surrendered the last organized Confederate troops in Arkansas, he eventually settled in New Orleans. Thompson tried numerous business ventures in the Crescent City, but they were uniformly unsuccessful. He did play an active role in the Republican party in Louisiana until the end of Reconstruction. Thompson died of tuberculosis on September 5, 1876, while visiting his family in St. Joseph, Missouri.

Thompson, William G.

Prior to the Civil War, Thompson had been a prominent attorney and had helped raise the 20th Iowa Infantry. His wound at Prairie Grove was severe, but he recovered in time to rejoin his regiment at Vicksburg. In 1864, Thompson resigned from the service because he had not fully recovered from his wound. He returned to Iowa, where he served as district attorney. In 1879, he was elected to Congress, and he served until 1883. From 1894 until 1906, Thompson served as judge of the 18th Federal Judicial District. He died on April 2, 1911, and was buried in Marion with many of his old comrades from the 20th Iowa.

Thomson, Tom D.

Thomson continued to serve with the 33d Arkansas Infantry until the end of the war. On April 15, 1864, the colonel of the regiment, H. L. Grinsted, was killed at Jenkins' Ferry, and Thomson, who was now a lieutenant colonel, assumed command. After the war, he returned to Camden where he clerked in a store until 1870 when he started his own business. In 1873, Thomson went bankrupt and returned to clerking. In 1889, he opened another store, and this one was successful. He was active in politics and in 1884 he was elected Ouachita County Clerk. He died in Camden on August 12, 1890.

Thrower, Christopher

"Kit" Thrower returned to Ouachita County after the war and edited a newspaper. In 1873 he was elected to a special session of the General Assembly. He later served two terms in the state senate. In 1877, he moved to Hot Springs where he practiced law and served as a judge. In 1883 he traveled to Little Rock, engaged rooms at the Adams House, and died on March 17, 1883. He was buried at Malvern.

Van Dorn, Earl

A few weeks after Pea Ridge, Van Dorn and his army were transferred to Mississippi. There he eventually commanded General John C. Pemberton's cavalry, a branch of the service that was perhaps more suited to his talents. In December, 1862, he scored a noteworthy success when he captured General Ulysses S. Grant's main supply depot at Holly Springs and temporarily disrupted the Union campaign against Vicksburg. On May 7, 1863, Van Dorn was in his headquarters at Spring Hill, Tennessee, when Dr. George B. Peters walked in and killed the general. For months, rumors had circulated among the townspeople about an affair between Van Dorn and Peters' young wife Jessie. Peters was eventually tried and acquitted. After the war, he did divorce his wife, but they remarried

and moved to Phillips County in Arkansas where he was elected later to the Arkansas state senate. Peters died in 1889, his wife in 1921.

Van Houten, Harry F.

When the war ended, Van Houten enlisted in the regular army, and retired in 1882 as sergeant major in the 14th United States Infantry. After his retirement from the service, Van Houten lived in Kansas City, Kansas, Fort Dodge, Kansas, and Quincy, Illinois. He died in Quincy on September 6, 1923, at the age of eighty-five.

Walker, David

After the secession convention, Walker played no role in the war until May 1, 1863, when he accepted a commission as colonel to serve on the military court in southern Arkansas. All four of his sons served in the Confederate armies, and one, Jacob Wythe, died at Jenkins' Ferry. After the war, Walker served three terms on the state supreme court. He died on September 30, 1879, from injuries received when he was thrown from a runaway buggy at the Washington County Fair.

Walker, Jacob Wythe

Wounded on April 30, 1864, at Jenkins' Ferry, Walker was nursed for almost a month by his father. Despite hopeful reports from David Walker to his family, Jacob Wythe died on May 31, 1864.

Warford, Francis B.

Warford was captured with Dockery's 19th Arkansas Infantry at Island No. 10. He and his unit were parolled, and then rejoined active Confederate service in time to be captured a second time at Vicksburg on July 4, 1863. At Vicksburg, Warford signed parole papers, his "x" indicating that he could not write. Warford was not involved in active service again, and apparently did not remain in Arkansas.

Watie, Stan

After Pea Ridge, Watie and his men fought primarily as raiders along the borders of the Indian Territory. Watie surrendered on June 23, 1865, and returned to his farm and business enterprises in the Territory. He died on September 9, 1871.

Weaver, Omer

Weaver was killed at Wilson's Creek on August 10, 1862.

White, R. H.

White accompanied Union forces to Arkansas in 1863, setting up his first studio at De Valls Bluff. He moved to Little Rock sometime in 1864. On January 21, 1864, the Quartermaster Corps issued General Order No. 3, which required each military district to photographically document the condition of all buildings constructed by the army. White received the contract for this work and produced most of the photographs of public buildings in Little Rock and De Valls Bluff which appear in this volume. The photos were forwarded to the quartermaster general on September 26, 1865. Shortly afterward White left Arkansas.

Wilkins, Willis Perry

Wilkins served in Company A, 29th Arkansas Infantry, throughout the war. After the war, he returned to Cross County where he was a planter. He was a prominent member of his community and active in politics. He served as constable of his township and as a member of the county school board. He was a Mason and a member of the Methodist Episcopal Church South. When he died on December 10, 1906, he was buried in his family cemetery alongside his old friend, Colonel David C. Cross.

Williamson, James A.

In April, 1862, Williamson was elected colonel of the 4th Iowa Infantry. He went on to fight at Chickasaw Bluffs, Arkansas Post, Lookout Mountain, Missionary Ridge, and Atlanta. Williamson was wounded five times, and mustered out of the service as a major general. After the war, he was involved in promoting railroads, and became president of the Atlantic and Pacific line. He died on September 7, 1902.

Wood, Walter

Wood mustered out of the army on February 12, 1866, and returned to Southfield, Michigan, where he married Mary E. Newman on May 23, 1866. Wood later moved to Detroit, and he worked as a miller until his health, which had been poor since contracting typhoid fever in 1863, began to fail. On February 28, 1892, Woods filed for permanent disability, citing heart and kidney disease, sunstroke, rheumatism, and partial paralysis of the right leg, but he was rejected. Wood continued to apply for a pension until May 15, 1909, when the federal government finally approved his request, and granted him fifteen dollars per month. He died in Detroit on December 26, 1915.

Word, William Buford

William Word was discharged from the 20th Arkansas Infantry on March 31, 1863, at the age of forty. The reason for his discharge was given as "old age." He was paid $105.35 in back salary and for transportation home from Camp Pritchard, Mississippi. He returned to his wife and four-year-old son in New Edinburgh, Bradley County. He farmed there until his death in 1875. He is buried at McCoy Cemetery in New Edinburgh.

Notes

Introduction

1. *Helena Shield,* 4 February 1860.

2. Dorothy Stanley, ed., *The Autobiography of Sir Henry Morton Stanley* (New York: Houghton-Mifflin Company, 1909), 171.

3. *Washington Telegraph,* 22 January 1862.

4. T. J. Gaughan, ed., *Letters of a Confederate Surgeon, 1861–1865* (Camden, Arkansas: Hurley, Co., 1960), 220–21.

5. (Fort Smith) *New Era,* 12 December 1863, 6 May 1864.

6. (Little Rock) *Unconditional Union,* 8 September 1864, 30 March, 6 April 1865.

7. *Ibid.,* 6 May 1864.

Chapter 1

1. Record Book, Van Buren Frontier Guards, 1861–May 17, 1864. Arkansas Miscellaneous Manuscripts. University of Arkansas at Little Rock, Archives and Special Collections.

2. Stanley, *The Autobiography of Sir Henry Morton Stanley,* 171.

3. Charlean Williams, *The Old Town Speaks: Washington, Hempstead County, Arkansas, Gatewood to Texas, 1835, Confederate Capital, 1863* (Houston: Anson Jones Press, 1951), 307.

4. *Appendix to the Congressional Globe,* 36th Cong., 1st Session, XXIX, 82.

5. John M. Harrell, "Arkansas," *Confederate Military History* (Atlanta: Confederate Publishing Company, 1899), X, 8.

6. David Walker to W. W. Mansfield, March 3, 1861, W. W. Mansfield Collection, Arkansas History Commission.

7. Jesse Cypert, "Reminiscences of the Secession Convention," *Papers of the Arkansas Historical Association,* I, 318.

8. *Ibid.,* 319.

9. *War of the Rebellion: Official Records of the Union and Confederate Armies,* 130 vols. (Washington D.C., Government Printing Office, 1880–1901), Ser. I, Vol. III, 123. (Hereafter referred to as *O.R.*)

10. Endorsement in Van Manning File, Combined Service Records, Third Arkansas Infantry (Confederate), National Archives.

Chapter 2

1. William H. Tunnard, *A Southern Record: The History of the Third Regiment, Louisiana Infantry* (Baton Rouge: Privately printed, 1866), 145.

2. Letter of General Curtis, March 13, 1862, quoted in Bruce Catton, *Terrible Swift Sword* (New York: Doubleday & Co., 1963), 223–24.

3. C. Barney, *Recollections of Field Service with the Twentieth Iowa Infantry Volunteers* (Davenport, Iowa: Privately printed, 1865), 131.

4. *Memphis Daily Appeal,* 4 March 1863.

5. Robert J. Hartje, *Van Dorn* (Nashville: Vanderbilt University Press, 1967), 100.

6. Return Ira Holcombe, *An Account of the Battle of Wilson's Creek or Oak Hills, Fought Between the Union Troops . . . and the Southern or Confederate Troops . . .* (Springfield, Missouri: Dow & Adams, 1883), 14.

7. *Ibid.,* 19.

8. Robert McCulloch to Sterling Price, November 29, 1861, Combined Service Record, Second Missouri Cavalry (Confederate), McCulloch, Robert, National Archives.

9. *O.R.,* Ser. I, Vol. VIII, 269.

10. Tunnard, *Southern Record,* 132–3.

11. *O.R.,* Ser. I, Vol. III, 107.

12. Tunnard, *Southern Record,* 135.

13. *O.R.,* Ser. I, Vol. XXII, 83.

14. Howard N. Monett, ed., "A Yankee Cavalryman Views the Battle of Prairie Grove," *Arkansas Historical Quarterly,* XXXVIII (Winter, 1962): 294.

15. Walter J. Lemke, ed., *Captain Edward Gee Miller of the 20th Wisconsin: His War, 1861–1865* (Fayetteville: Washington County Historical Society, 1960), 12.

16. *O.R.,* Ser. I, Vol. III, 140, 154.

17. Tom Thomson to Dear Sisters, December 15, 1862, in M. A. Elliot, comp., *The Garden of Memory* (Camden, Arkansas: Brown Printing Co., 1911), 69.

18. William Thompson to Dear Wife, December 10, 1862, in Edwin C. Bearss, ed., *The Civil War Letters of Major William G. Thompson of the 20th Iowa Regiment* (Fayetteville: Washington County Historical Society, 1966), 89–91.

19. S. C. Turnbo, "History of the 27th Arkansas Confederate Regiment" (Unpublished diary, J. N. Heiskell Historical Collection, University of Arkansas at Little Rock, Archives and Special Collections), 152, 153, 202.

Chapter 3

1. *O.R.,* Ser. I, Vol. XIII, 835.

2. John Brown Diary, July 6, 1862, Arkansas History Commission.

3. *O.R.,* Ser. I, Vol. XII, 38.

4. Arthur Marvin Shaw, ed., "A Texas Ranger Company at the Battle of Arkansas Post," *Arkansas Historical Quarterly,* IX (Winter 1950): 289.

5. *Ibid.*

6. Florence Marie Ankeny Cox, ed., *Kiss Josey For Me* (Santa Anna, California: Friis-Pioneer Press, 1974), 86.

7. (Little Rock) *Patriot,* 28 March 1863.

8. Robert S. Waterman and Thomas Rothrock, eds., "The Earle-Buchanan Letters of 1861–1876," *Arkansas Historical Quarterly,* XXXIII (Summer 1974): 137.

9. *O.R.,* Ser. I, Vol. XVII, 781.

10. *Ibid.,* 782.

11. *Ibid.,* Ser. I, Vol. XXII, pt. 1, 409.

12. "Benjamin F. Pearson's War Diary," *Annals of Iowa,* Third Series, vol. 15 (October 1925), no. 2, 101–2.

13. George M. Blackburn, ed., *"Dear Carrie . . .": The Civil War Letters of Thomas N. Stevens* (Mount Pleasant, Mich.: Clarke Historical Library/Central Michigan University, 1984), 43.

14. *Ibid.,* 94–5.

15. *O.R.,* Ser. I, Vol. XXII, pt. 1, 432.

16. Minos Miller to Dear Mother, July 6, 1863, Minos Miller Papers, Special Collections, David Mullins Library, University of Arkansas at Fayetteville.

17. *O.R.,* Ser. I, Vol. XXII, pt. 1, 400.

18. Blackburn, *"Dear Carrie . . .",* 127.

Chapter 4

1. E. L. Pelton to D. B. I. Sterrett, March 7, 1863, aboard gunboat Conestoga, Miscellaneous Letter Collection, University of Arkansas at Little Rock, Archives and Special Collections.

2. *Official Records of the Union and Confederate Navies in the War of the Rebellion,* 7 vols. (Washington, D.C.: Government Printing Office, 1912), Ser. I, Vol. 25, 354.

3. *Ibid.,* Ser. I, Vol. 23, 166, 169.

4. Henry Walke, "The Gun-boats at Belmont and Fort Henry," *Battles and Leaders of the Civil War* (New York: Castle Books, 1956), I, 359.

Chapter 5

1. Asa S. Morgan to Dear Wife, September 26, 1863, A. S. Morgan Papers, Arkansas History Commission.

2. Francis Mitchell Ross, ed., "Civil War Letters from James Mitchell to His Wife—Sarah Elizabeth Mitchell," *Arkansas Historical Quarterly,* XXXVII (Winter 1978): 314.

3. Gaughan, ed., *Letters of a Confederate Surgeon,* 121.

4. *O.R.,* Ser. I, Vol. XXII, 518.

5. B. T. Simmons to Dear Sisters, September 27, 1863, Miscellaneous Letter Collection, University of Arkansas at Little Rock, Archives and Special Collections.

6. John D. Billings, *Hardtack and Coffee* (Boston: George Smith & Co, 1887), 252–53.

7. *Ibid.,* 281, 286.

8. *Ibid.,* 282–87.

9. George M. Blackburn, *"Dear Carrie . . .",* 277.

10. A. F. Sperry, *History of the 33d Iowa Volunteer Infantry* (Des Moines: Mills & Co., 1866), 105.

Chapter 6

1. W. L. Gammage, *The Camp, The Bivouac, and the Battle Field* (Selma, Alabama, n.p., 1864), 16.

2. J. P. Blessington, *The Campaigns of Walker's Texas Division* (New York: Lange, Little & Co., 1875), 44.

3. Gaughan, *Letters of a Confederate Surgeon,* 102.

4. Turnbo, "History of the Twenty-Seventh Arkansas," 224.

5. William Baxter, *Pea Ridge and Prairie Grove* (Cincinnati: Poe & Hitchcock, 1864), 188, 191.

6. Ruie Ann Smith Park, ed., "Dear Parents," *The Civil War Letters of the Shibley Brothers of Van Buren, Arkansas* (Fayetteville, Arkansas: Washington County Historical Society, 1963), Letter No. 42.

7. Gaughan, *Letters of a Confederate Surgeon,* 128.

8. *O.R.,* Ser. I, Vol. XLI, pt. 2, 714.

9. Leander Stillwell, *The Story of a Common Soldier of Army Life in the Civil War* (Erie, Kansas: Erie Press, 1917), 84–5.

10. Sperry, *History of the 33d Iowa Volunteer Regiment,* 41.

11. *O.R.,* Ser. I, Vol. XLI, pt. 2, 220.

12. *Ibid.,* Ser. I, Vol. XLVIII, pt. 2, 31–2.

13. Gaughan, *Letters of a Confederate Surgeon,* 183.

14. Combined Service Records, Fourth Arkansas Infantry (Confederate), McCollum, John N. National Archives.

Chapter 7

1. F. Heineman, "The Federal Occupation of Camden as Set Forth in the Diary of a Union Soldier," *Arkansas Historical Quarterly,* IX (Autumn 1950): 216.

2. *Ibid.*

3. "Benjamin F. Pearson's War Diary," *Annals of Iowa,* Third Series, Vol. 16 (Oct. 1926): no. 2, 441.

4. Heineman, "The Federal Occupation of Camden . . .", 219.

5. Ralph R. Rea, ed., "Diary of Private John P. Wright, U.S.A., 1864–1865," *Arkansas Historical Quarterly,* XVI (Autumn 1957): 317.

6. Isaac Murphy to Abraham Lincoln, May 11, 1864, Murphy/Berry Papers, Arkansas History Commission.

7. Harold F. Lupold, ed., "An Ohio Doctor Views Campaigning on the White River, 1864," *Arkansas Historical Quarterly,* XXXIV (Winter 1975): 348.

8. Edgar Langsdorf, ed., "The Letters of Joseph H. Trego, 1857–1864, Linn County Pioneer," *Kansas Historical Quarterly,* XIX (November 1951): 399.

9. *O.R.,* Ser. I, Vol. XXXIV, pt. 1, 659.

10. J. William Demby, "A History of the Third Missouri Cavalry," April 12, 1864, 70. Unpublished manuscript, University of Arkansas at Little Rock, Archives and Special Collections.

11. *O.R.,* Ser. I, Vol. XXXIV, pt. 1, 671.

12. Gaughan, *Letters of a Confederate Surgeon,* 227–28.

13. *O.R.,* Ser. I, Vol. XXXIV, pt. 1, 800.

14. Photograph Collection, University of Arkansas at Little Rock, Archives and Special Collections.

15. *O.R.,* Series I, Vol. XXXIV, pt. 1, 33.

16. *Ibid.,* Ser. I, Vol. XLI, pt. 1, 191.

17. *Ibid.,* Ser. I, Vol. LX, pt. 1, 230.

18. *Ibid.,* 237.

Chapter 8

1. Gammage, *The Camp, the Bivouac, and the Battlefield* (Selma: n.p., 1864), 106.

2. Joe M. Scott, *Four Years' Service in the Confederate Army* (First published at Mulberry, Arkansas, 1897, reprinted by the Washington County Historical Society, 1958), 49.

3. "United Confederate Veterans," *Confederate Veteran,* I (January, 1893): 11.

4. *Ibid.*

5. Mary Barnett Poppenheim, *The History of the United Daughters of the Confederacy* (Richmond: Garrett and Massie, 1938), 11.

6. B. A. C. Emerson (comp.), *Historic Southern Monuments* (New York: Neal Publishing Co., 1911), 55, 57, 63.

7. *Journal of the Twenty-First Annual Encampment, Department of Arkansas, Grand Army of the Republic, held at Mammoth Spring, May 19, 1903,* Appendix, p. 11.

8. *Arkansas Gazette,* 31 May 1913.

9. United States War Department, Adjutant General's Office, *Amnesty Papers, Arkansas,* Record Group 94.

10. James M. Hanks Diary, September 28, 1868, Phillips County Museum.

11. Daniel Harvey Reynolds Diary, April 20, 1865, xerox copy in Special Collections, David Mullins Library, University of Arkansas at Fayetteville.

12. *Ibid.,* June 14, 1865.

Bibliography

Introduction

Brady, Mathew B. "Interview with George Alfred Town-send." *New York World,* April 12, 1891, p. 23.

Cobb, Josephine. "Alexander Gardner." *Image: Journal of Photography,* VII (June 1956): 124–36.

———. "Photographers of the Civil War." *Military Affairs* 26 (Fall 1962): 127–35.

Davis, William C., ed. *The Image of War, 1861–1865.* 6 vols. New York: Doubleday & Company, Inc., 1981.

Frassanito, William A. *Gettysburg: A Journey in Time.* New York: Scribner, 1975.

———. *Antietam: The Photographic Legacy of America's Bloodiest Day.* New York: Scribner, 1978.

Gardner, Alexander. *Sketchbook of the War (1865).* New York: Dover, 1959.

Gladstone, William. "Captain Andrew J. Russell: First Army Photographer." *Photographica* 10 (February 1978): 7–9.

Horan, James D. *Mathew Brady: Historian With a Camera.* New York: Bonanza Books, 1955.

Meredith, Roy. *Mr. Lincoln's Camera Man: Mathew B. Brady.* New York: Dover Publications, Inc., 1974.

Miller, Francis Treveyn, ed. *Photographic History of the War.* New York: The Review of Reviews Co., 1912.

Taft, Robert. *Photography and the American Scene, A Social History.* New York: Macmillan, 1938.

Chapter 1

Dougan Michael B. *Confederate Arkansas: The People and Policies of a Frontier State in Wartime.* University: The University of Alabama Press, 1976.

Ferguson, John L., ed. *Arkansas and the Civil War.* Little Rock: Pioneer Press, 1962.

Harrell, John M. *Confederate Military History.* Vol. X. Atlanta: Confederate Publishing Company, 1899.

Stanley, Dorothy, ed. *The Autobiography of Sir Henry Morton Stanley.* New York: Houghton Mifflin Company, 1909.

Thomas, David Y. *Arkansas in War and Reconstruction, 1861–1874.* Little Rock: Arkansas Division, United Daughters of the Confederacy, 1926.

Chapter 2

Bearss, Edwin C. "The First Day at Pea Ridge, March 7, 1862." *Arkansas Historical Quarterly* XVII (Summer 1958): 119–31.

———. "From Rolla to Fayetteville with General Curtis." *Arkansas Historical Quarterly* XIX (Autumn 1960): 225–59.

Brown, Walter. "Pea Ridge: Gettysburg of the West." *Arkansas Historical Quarterly* XV (Spring 1956): 3–16.

Monnett, Howard N. "A Yankee Cavalryman Views the Battle of Prairie Grove." *Arkansas Historical Quarterly* XXI (Winter 1962): 289–304.

Oates, Stephen B. "The Prairie Grove Campaign, 1862." *Arkansas Historical Quarterly* XIX (Summer 1960): 119–41.

Chapter 3

Bearss, Edwin C. "The Battle of Helena, July 4, 1863." *Arkansas Historical Quarterly* XX (Autumn 1961): 256–98.

Reynolds, Donald E. "Union Strategy in Arkansas During the Vicksburg Campaign." *Arkansas Historical Quarterly* XXIX (Spring 1970): 20–38.

Shaw, Arthur Marvin, ed. "A Texas Ranger Company at the Battle of Arkansas Post." *Arkansas Historical Quarterly* IX (Winter 1950): 270–97.

Waterman, Robert E., and Thomas Rhothrock. "The Earle-Buchanan Letters of 1861–1876." *Arkansas Historical Quarterly* XXXIII (Summer 1974): 99–174.

Chapter 4

Gosnell, H. Allen. *Guns on the Western Waters: The Story of River Gunboats in the Civil War.* Baton Rouge: Louisiana State University Press, 1949.

Merrill, James M. *Battle Flags South: The Story of the Civil War Navies on Western Waters.* Rutherford: Fairleigh Dickenson University Press, 1970.

Milligan, John D. *Gunboats Down the Mississippi.* Annapolis: U.S. Naval Institute, 1965.

Chapter 5

Bearss, Edwin C. "The Battle of the Post of Arkansas." *Arkansas Historical Quarterly* XVIII (Autumn 1959): 237–79.

Cowen, Ruth Caroline. "Reorganization of Federal Arkansas, 1862–1865." *Arkansas Historical Quarterly* XVIII (Summer 1959): 32–57.

Huff, Leo E. "The Union Expedition Against Little Rock, August-September, 1863." *Arkansas Historical Quarterly* XII (Fall 1963): 224–37.

———. "The Last Duel in Arkansas: The Marmaduke-Walker Duel." *Arkansas Historical Quarterly* XXIII (Spring 1964): 36–49.

———. "The Memphis and Little Rock Railroad During the Civil War." *Arkansas Historical Quarterly* XXIII (Autumn 1964): 260–70.

Ross, Francis Mitchell. "Civil War Letters from James Mitchell to His Wife, Sarah Elizabeth Latta Mitchell." *Arkansas Historical Quarterly* XXXVII (Winter, 1978): 306–17.

Chapter 6

Brooks, Steward. *Civil War Medicine.* Springfield: C. C. Thomas & Co., 1966.

Cunningham, Horace H. *Doctors in Gray.* Baton Rouge: Louisiana State University Press, 1958.

Steiner, Paul E. *Disease in the Civil War.* Springfield: C. C. Thomas & Co., 1968.

Chapter 7

Atkinson, J. H. "The Action at Prairie De Ann." *Arkansas Historical Quarterly* XIX (Spring 1960): 46–50.

Bearss, Edwin C. "The Federals Struggle to Hold on to Fort Smith." *Arkansas Historical Quarterly* XXIV (Summer 1965): 149–79.

Heinemann, F. "The Federal Occupation of Camden as Set Forth in the Diary of a Union Officer." *Arkansas Historical Quarterly* IX (Autumn 1950): 214–19.

Hunsicker, Neva Ingram. "Rayburn the Raider." *Arkansas Historical Quarterly* VII (Spring 1948): 87–91.

Langsdorf, Edgar, ed. "The Letters of Joseph H. Trego, 1857–1864, Linn County Pioneer." *Kansas Historical Quarterly* 19 (November, 1951, August 1951): 287–309, 381–400.

Loupold, Harry Forrest, ed. "An Ohio Doctor Views Campaigning in the White River, 1864." *Arkansas Historical Quarterly* 34 (Winter 1975): 333–51.

———. "Benjamin F. Pearson's War Diary," *Annals of Iowa,* 15 (1925–27), 83–129, 194–222, 281–306, 377–90, 433–63, 507–35.

Rhea, Ralph R. "Diary of Private John P. Wright, U.S.A., 1864–1865." *Arkansas Historical Quarterly* XVI (Autumn 1957): 304–18.

Richards, Ira Don. "The Battle of Poison Spring." *Arkansas Historical Quarterly* XVIII (Winter 1959): 338–49.

———. "The Engagement at Marks' Mills." *Arkansas Historical Quarterly* XIX (Spring 1960): 51–60.

———. "The Battle of Jenkins' Ferry." *Arkansas Historical Quarterly* XX (Spring 1961): 3–16.

Shea, William L. "Battle at Ditch Bayou." *Arkansas Historical Quarterly* XXXIX (Autumn 1980): 195–207.

Worley, Ted R., ed. "Diary of Lieutenant Orville Gillet, U.S.A., 1864–1865." *Arkansas Historical Quarterly* XVII (Summer 1985): 164–204.

Chapter 8

Hesseltine, William B., and Larry Gara. "'Arkansas' Confederate Leaders After the War." *Arkansas Historical Quarterly* IX (Winter, 1950): 259–69.

Index

241